HOMES
& GARDENS
Decorating

STYLE ADVICE • DESIGN OPTIONS • PRACTICAL KNOW-HOW

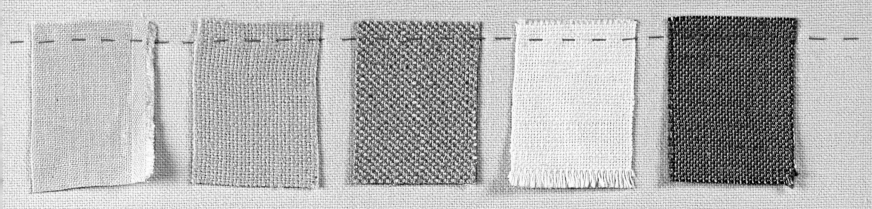

HOMES & GARDENS

Decorating

STYLE ADVICE • DESIGN OPTIONS • PRACTICAL KNOW-HOW

Giles Kime

First published in 2006 by
Conran Octopus Limited
a part of Octopus Publishing Group
2–4 Heron Quays, London E14 4JP
www.conran-octopus.co.uk

Publishing Director: Lorraine Dickey
Executive Editor: Zia Mattocks
Editors: Sybella Marlow, Emma Clegg
Art Director: Jonathan Christie
Designer: Barbara Zuñiga
Picture Research Manager: Liz Boyd
Picture Researcher: Jess Walton
Production Manager: Angela Young

ISBN 1 84091 446 7
Printed in China

Homes & Gardens is a trade mark of IPC Media
© IPC Media Limited 2006

To subscribe to *Homes & Gardens* magazine call 0845 6767778
or click on www.ipcmedia.com

Contents

Introduction

Why should we want to decorate the places where we live? For many of us it's simply because they are an intimate personal expression of who we are.

Our homes are more than just bricks and mortar; they also play a pivotal role in our emotional and physical lives. They are where we live out a vast proportion of our daily lives – sleeping, cooking, eating, bathing, entertaining and, in many cases, working. Added to that is the fact that for most of us our homes are the biggest investments that we ever make, so while we want to create an environment that we like, we also hope that someone else will like it when we come to sell.

UNDERSTANDING THE PROBLEMS

For all these reasons the way we decorate our homes will have an impact on many aspects of our lives. And it is because of the apparent enormity of that task that an activity which should be pleasurable can seem like an awesome, almost insurmountable hurdle. But the problem is not just satisfying our expectations and those of others; there is no doubt that when we plan a decorating project, many of us are flummoxed by the huge number of choices on offer – a seemingly infinite array of furniture, fabrics, wallpapers, flooring and accessories. The possibilities are sometimes so numerous that it seems easier just to create an anonymous scheme – or, worse still, to do nothing at all. Another commonly encountered problem is the fact that when it comes to interior design many of us lack faith in our own opinions. While we will happily discuss our favourite food, music or movies, we are less forthcoming when the subject is fabrics, paint colours or a style of chair.

DECORATING MADE EASY

The purpose of this book is to take the fear out of the decorating process. It isn't necessary to trawl though every paint and fabric on the market. Instead, one simply needs to look at the broad range of styles on offer and decide which appeal to you most. Doing so will hugely reduce the number of

OPPOSITE A combination of simple flooring and elaborate upholstery strike a stylish balance of old and new in this Regency house in Hampshire. It is a good example of how period detail can look surprisingly modern when given the right treatment.

options you'll have to consider and within days you'll have before you a selection of choices that roughly approximate to the look that you'd like to achieve. The idea is not that you set out to slavishly copy them, but rather that they help you get an idea of what is possible. The best interior design is not necessarily about creating something that is completely new but taking an existing idea and making it your own.

TRUSTING YOUR INSTINCTS

In the early chapters you'll be encouraged to compare and contrast colours, patterns and textures to create combinations that will work beautifully. By a process of elimination, you'll come to understand what you do and don't like, and what does and doesn't sit happily together. Better still, because you have seen them side by side, you won't be in for any unexpected surprises. You'll also explore the most prevalent styles as well as the functions of each room in the house, allowing you to marry both practicality and aesthetics. Every aspect of the decorating process is considered, from finding inspiration and planning to subjects such as paint, wallpaper and panelling. The final chapter gives invaluable guidance on some of the basic practical tasks such as painting, tiling, wallpapering and making curtains.

Having worked your way through from beginning to end, you'll not only be equipped with all the skills required to create a room that fulfils your needs and appeals to your tastes – but also, more importantly, you should believe in your own opinions.

OPPOSITE Here, a combination of texture linen and a deep pile rug lend a soft, comfortable look to this otherwise simple interior. Combining different fabrics in the same chair and cushion create a discreetly decorative style.

1

Finding a Style

One of the hardest, most time-consuming tasks in any decorating project is not wallpapering, scraping down paint or upholstering a chair but finding a style that suits you, your home and the intended purpose of the room.

This chapter is designed to demonstrate the range of available styles that might appeal. But these suggestions are not meant to be prescriptive: each of the ten most popular decorating styles explored on the following pages is intended simply as a snapshot of what is possible. The most successful decorating schemes – and those that we are most likely to feel comfortable in – are the ones that recognize our personal tastes and needs. So use the decorating styles shown here to direct you towards a general visual emphasis that you can then interpret in your own way.

THIS PAGE The minimal style is particularly well suited to functional rooms such as kitchens and bathrooms. In this simple bathroom, storage has been banished to create a look that is clean, simple and practical.

OPPOSITE Low-level built-in cupboards in an open-plan dining area provide plenty of storage for the necessities of everyday life.

Minimal

To achieve a minimal look you need to be rigorous – and to learn that less is definitely more.

Minimalism in its purest form has its roots in the architecture of Japan's Buddhist monasteries. In the 1980s the principles of Japanese minimalism were applied to domestic interiors, creating a style characterized by beautifully simple rooms that contained little but crisp, white surfaces. One of the main advantages of minimalism is that it can lend even the darkest room a light, uplifting feel. It is particularly well suited to rooms where there is a specific activity, such as a kitchen or bathroom, in which it is important to make the best possible use of space. Because the look relies on the absence of all but the most essential items of furniture, it relies on a rigorous approach to tidiness as well as plenty of storage, that will add substantially to the total cost of the project. Remember, too, that rooms decorated in a very minimal style will be much noisier than those filled with furniture, fabric and carpets, which have the advantage of absorbing sound.

KEY INGREDIENTS

* **Walls** Off-white paint or polished plaster
* **Floors** Wood, painted concrete, linoleum, rubber
* **Windows** Shutters or blinds
* **Upholstery** Plain neutrals

* **Walls** Neutral paint colours, textured wallpapers or wallpapers depicting simple graphic patterns
* **Floors** Textured carpet, wood, limestone
* **Windows** Curtains and blinds in fabric such as linen, velvet and chenille
* **Upholstery** Textured fabrics such as linen, chenille and velvet

ABOVE Built-in seating makes good use of space and creates useful extra storage.

ABOVE RIGHT Soften the hard, crisp edges of the modern look with heavy, textured fabrics.

OPPOSITE The clean lines of a Shaker-style table mix well with these simple modern chairs.

Liveable Modern

This sleek marriage of old and new offers you the best of both worlds.

For those who are attracted to the clean lines of minimalism combined with the comfort and convenience of a traditional interior, this look offers an excellent compromise. Its essence lies in the combination of a spare, contemporary style with heavily textured fabrics and floorcoverings that make it ideal for living rooms and bedrooms. The furniture has a sleek, modern feel and walls are often covered with richly coloured textured wallpaper or paint. Because furniture tends to be large to accommodate this style it is important to pay attention to the use of space and the style tends to works best in open-plan rooms. And, just like the minimal look, it relies on plenty of unobtrusive storage. Good lighting is key; so for the best results consider a combination of recessed, low-voltage spotlights and contemporary table and standard lamps. Because the look is spare and architectural, pay attention to the quality of finishes – as ever, the beauty lies in the details.

Simple

For many people, a simple scheme is the perfect way to combine good looks with practicality.

KEY INGREDIENTS

* **Walls** Soft, muted paint colours, simple panelling
* **Floors** Painted floors, natural flooring such as seagrass, coir and sisal
* **Windows** Blinds, shutters or simple curtains in plains or simple florals
* **Upholstery** Plain cotton or linen
* **Furniture** A combination of 'utility' furniture and simple upholstered furniture

ABOVE A trestle table and a pair of 'cricket pavilion' chairs are all that are required to create a calm environment in which to work.

ABOVE LEFT A combination of painted floorboards and tongue-and-groove panelling offers an inexpensive option for a bathroom.

OPPOSITE A pair of vibrantly coloured curtains and a lampshade in a similar hue have been used to add a fresh look to an otherwise neutral interior.

If only this style of decorating was as easy to create as the name suggests. In fact, achieving a simple look is a far more complex business than creating an elaborate one. As with minimalism, the challenge isn't just to achieve perfect finishes, but also that the beauty of this look is in the details. What distinguishes simplicity from minimalism is the subtle use of colour and quirky touches which are essential to the style. With a simple style it is the almost imperceptible details, such as buttons on upholstery and simple wall panelling, that lift the look beyond being stark and utilitarian. Paint colours tend to be fresh but muted, such as duck-egg blues and sage greens. Plain linens are ideal for curtains and upholstery – as well as stripes and simple, two-colour florals. For floors, paint or natural flooring, such as coir, seagrass or sisal, are popular options.

Country Cottage

In its new incarnation, the rustic style is perfect for creating a discreetly decorative scheme.

KEY INGREDIENTS

* **Walls** Creams and off-whites
* **Floors** Terracotta for kitchens, carpet and natural flooring for the rest of the house
* **Windows** Simple floral pleated curtains on wooden poles or simple pelmets
* **Upholstery** Florals, linens or simple checks

RIGHT Grouping collections of items in the same colours is a key part of this simple, comfortable look.

OPPOSITE An example of how paint and bed linen in a neutral palette of colours can be used to give a calm, soothing feel to a rustic interior.

In recent years this once fussy, cluttered style has been simplified to suit modern tastes. Instead of heavy oak furniture and busy floral fabrics the look is more likely to consist of painted furniture scaled down to suit the limited confines of small rooms. And while the essential ingredients, such as dressers (hutches) and other pieces of country-style furniture, are still centre-stage, a combination of a significantly pared-down approach and the use of pale colours for floors, walls and woodwork have made the look much more suited to modern tastes. It is the perfect option for those with a magpie's instinct for collecting as it relies on pretty decorative accessories, particularly china. But it isn't necessary to live in a country cottage in order to choose this look – it is perfect for a variety of other architectural styles and is a popular option for both kitchens and bedrooms.

Casual French

The rich colours and textures of the French country look create a warm, inviting feel.

For a country style with a difference, look to provincial France for inspiration. In comparison with the English rustic style this is a little more elegant – the furniture tends to be more ornate and the colours richer. Think of the colours of the Provençal countryside: the deep terracottas, sage greens, umbers and yellow ochres are also reflected in the domestic interiors of the region. Typical fabrics for this look are ginghams as well as distinctive Provençal fabrics from French markets that come in vibrant primary colours. France's association with gastronomy make this look perfect for kitchens – and the increasingly popular combined kitchen and dining room. The most characteristic furniture in this style is painted, or you could consider playing on the rustic theme by opting for a distressed finish. Alternatively, choose richly coloured polished woods. Complete the look with earthy Provençal ceramics and robust table linen.

KEY INGREDIENTS

* **Walls** Terracotta, umber, duck-egg blue
* **Floors** Terracotta for kitchens, stripped wooden floors
* **Windows** Simple pleated curtains in Provençal fabrics
* **Upholstery** Heavy linens

OPPOSITE A combination of metal furniture, stone flooring and a typical Provençal yellow have been used to create a relaxed French feel.
BELOW LEFT Linen tablecloths, checked seat pads and a rustic hanging light give this dining room a provincial French flavour.
BELOW Brass fittings, terracotta floors and panelled walls create a simple yet sophisticated look.

Classic French

The formality of 18th-century French interiors offers the perfect way to create an elegant look.

- **Walls** Off-white, jade, duck-egg blue. Real or fake panelling
- **Floors** Parquet, stripped or painted floors, Aubusson-style carpets or rugs
- **Windows** Toile de Jouy curtains, silk, hard pelmet
- **Upholstery** Toile de Jouy, silk, velvet or linen

This look is much grander in style than French country and more redolent of a neo-classical Loire château than a Provençal farmhouse. But you don't need to opt for the complete look with 'Louis-style' everything from armchairs to marble fireplaces. Instead, choose a few key pieces that will create the suggestion of the style without necessarily completely re-creating it. The elegant simplicity of classic French furniture mixes well with contemporary furniture, particularly when the latter is painted or upholstered in plain colours (or, for the classic look, choose toile de Jouy or silk). Panelling – either real or fake – offers the perfect backdrop, but a simple contemporary setting can work equally well. The ideal flooring is parquet with Aubusson-style rugs for a truly authentic feel. Alternatively, consider natural flooring or painted wood. Elaborate chandeliers – particularly crystal – will finish the look.

ABOVE Furniture decorated with intricate carving is a key ingredient of a formal French style.
ABOVE LEFT Panelled walls not only offer an elegant backdrop but also provide an opportunity to manipulate the proportions of a room.
OPPOSITE An ornate bed inspired by an 18th-century original is the epitome of elegant French style. A toile de Jouy bedcover completes the look.

Classic Swedish

This fresh, crisp interior style is guaranteed to maximize the natural light in any room.

KEY INGREDIENTS

* **Walls** Off-white, jade, duck-egg blue, real or fake panelling
* **Floors** Stripped floors or painted floors, natural flooring, striped or checked rugs
* **Windows** Large checks, gingham, plain linens, hard pelmet
* **Upholstery** Large checks, plain linen

ABOVE RIGHT A simple wooden sofa softened with an upholstered seat pad and cushions is a familiar ingredient of a classic Swedish style.

OPPOSITE Another characteristic element is checked fabric and wallpaper, here adding a crisp look to this formal dining room. Co-ordinating tableware completes the look.

This popular look is inspired by the 18th- and 19th-century interiors in which classically inspired furniture offsets the simplicity of its surroundings. For inspiration, look at the charming depictions of domestic scenes created by Swedish artist Carl Larsson at the end of the 19th century. Because this look has a palette of pale colours such as soft greys, blue and greens – both for furniture and walls – it is ideal for rooms where light needs to be maximized. In extreme cases, a Swedish style offers the opportunity to create very pale interiors that don't seem too stark. The look has much in common with a classic French style but is slightly more austere. For windows, consider using shutters or curtains in plains, large checks or transparent voiles that make the most of any available light. When selecting finishes for floors consider stripped or painted floors – or go for the more comfortable option of natural flooring.

Classic English

This timeless style is ideal for combining comfort with classic good looks.

The classic English look has its origins in the interiors of grand English country houses during the first half of the 20th century, characterized by a combination of large, comfortable upholstered furniture, curtains in large-scale floral chintzes, 18th-century antiques, painted furniture and decorative paint finishes. However, by the 1980s this interior style became overbearing with the use of overly fussy curtain treatments and complex combinations of fabrics. In its new incarnation the country-house style has gone back to its roots; the look is now much cleaner and tends to rely on the combination of just one simple, dominant, large-scale floral and a the use of plain fabrics in cool colours. The result is that the look is now much easier to achieve, more affordable and more faithful to its original.

KEY INGREDIENTS

* **Walls** Floral wallpaper. Creams, neutrals or yellows for living rooms, deep reds and terracottas for dining rooms, soft pastels for bedrooms
* **Floors** Carpets, natural flooring, polished wood floors, Persian or Oriental carpets
* **Windows** Elaborate curtains in large-scale florals and checks
* **Upholstery** Linens, velvets and chenilles

OPPOSITE A combination of antique mahogany furniture, an antique gilded mirror and walls lined with a simple floral fabric give this country dining room a smart but comfortable feel.
LEFT A buttoned leather armchair, an imposing tallboy and a carved mirror lend this living room a more formal quality.

* **Walls** White and off-white or deep reds and browns
* **Floors** Dark wood floors, natural flooring, limestone, plain rugs
* **Windows** Blinds in neutral coloured fabrics
* **Upholstery** Dark coloured textured plains

OPPOSITE A good example of how contemporary furniture and ethnic accessories can be combined to create a sleek, exotic look.

BELOW Lacquer furniture, lighting and accessories have been used to create a dramatic look in this home office.

East Meets West

Create a cool, zen-like feel by blending the contemporary and the exotic.

This look combines the simplicity of Western-style minimalism with the calm, soothing style of Oriental interiors. A mix of sleek, modern designs such as large, low sofas with Oriental furniture and accessories are set against a plain, white backdrop. For a more striking look choose a colour setting of deep, moody hues. Whatever type of furniture you opt for, ensure that, regardless of the material, the predominant colours are blacks, browns and deep reds. Lacquer furniture and accessories, both new and antique, are integral to the style. For floors, the best options are stone or natural flooring. Large indoor plants, scented candles, joss sticks and water features help to enhance the exotic feel. For anyone wishing to create a calm, serene environment, particularly in a bedroom or bathroom, this look is the natural choice.

Exotic

The decorative style of exotic furniture creates
a look that will transport you to far-flung lands.

The combination of ornate furniture, decorative textiles and handmade accessories from India and the Far East creates a look that offers a form of escapism to those living in the West. There is no reason, however, why this style should fall into a hippyish Seventies-style cliché; by keeping the look spare and confining the choice of furniture to simpler designs, the appearance can be rich and seductive without being overbearing. For a colonial feel, use furniture with a European influence and choose cream fabrics for curtains and upholstery. For a more discreet look, mix elements of the style with traditional or contemporary designs that have a sleeker finish. To pull the look together successfully simply ensure that elements have a similar colour, regardless of their material.

ABOVE Simple accessories such as this inlaid box are a simple and often inexpensive means of creating an exotic look.
LEFT Items such as this oriental wardrobe help not only to create the look but also offer practical storage.
OPPOSITE Combining oriental style, pattern and furniture with neutral upholstery will create a softer, more contemporary feel than a palette of rich colours.

Mixing Styles

Create an eclectic look by combining furniture from different periods, textures and materials.

An increasingly popular option when planning a decorating scheme is to combine different styles, such as modern with traditional or European with Oriental. With this approach the secret is to ensure that different items of furniture and accessories – however diverse in style – have similar colours and textures; for instance, if you are mixing a mahogany Georgian console table with a contemporary sofa, make sure that the latter is upholstered in a fabric that is similar in tone.

When planning to decorate a number of rooms there is no need to stick to a single style throughout. You might find that there are some styles that are suited to certain rooms but don't work in others; so while classic English might be the ideal choice for your living room, minimalist may be a more effective option for a functional room such as a kitchen.

OPPOSITE A simple colour scheme ensures the combination of a classic religious painting and a pair of modernist chairs sit happily side-by-side.

BELOW Here an Indian table looks sleek and contemporary amid a scheme consisting of a cool combination of cream and purple.

KEY INGREDIENTS

* Ensure that colours of old and new items work together.
* If mixing styles in adjacent rooms try to create continuity with flooring or paint colours.
* If using antique furniture in a contemporary environment, ensure that it is as sleek and simple as possible.
* A good way to mix old and new is to upholster an antique piece of furniture in a contemporary fabric. Alternatively, you could upholster a traditional piece of furniture in contemporary fabric.

ABOVE Thanks to their similar colours, an 18th century-style clock sits quite happily next to an oriental style pattern.
ABOVE RIGHT A quirky wallpaper design lends an exotic look to an otherwise cohesive collection of furniture and accessories.
OPPOSITE By keeping colours the same, this kitchen sits quite happily alongside a more classic living room.

Similarly, if the feminine look of classic French is the one for your bedroom, you might decide that you want the calmer feel of a simple style in an en-suite bathroom. Another reason for mixing styles is that you can allow yourself to be led by the individual architectural styles of various rooms. For instance, if you have a contemporary extension that has been added to a traditionally decorated house, you might decide that it makes sense to furnish it in a simple, modern way.

When mixing styles between rooms, ensure that you find an effective way to relate one space to another. In the case of an adjoining bedroom and bathroom that are decorated in different styles, try to use the same flooring and colour scheme throughout – or at least one that is very similar in tone. This acts as a consistent element to smooth the transition. The progression from one room and one style to another should always be gradual rather than dramatic. It is for this reason that if you have a number of neighbouring rooms – for example a bathroom, living room and dining room – in two or three different styles, try to keep the hall and corridors as simple as possible.

2

Evolution or Revolution?

There are two approaches to any decorating project. One is to
allow it to 'evolve', a process that will typically start with painting
or papering the walls before tackling the floor, windows and
upholstery. For the inexperienced, this process of 'feeling your way'
from one element of a scheme to another has the advantage of
offering less fear of the unknown and of allowing you to spread
the cost of a project over a long period. The second approach is
'revolution', a process that involves starting with a blank canvas
for which everything from fabrics to lighting will be chosen, or
working around a few existing items of furniture. There isn't a
right or a wrong way to approach the subject. Your decision will
be influenced by a number of factors, such as your budget and
the extent to which you wish to use existing flooring and items
of furniture. Whichever of these two routes you choose, the
starting point should be the same – a phase of detailed planning.

THIS PAGE A dual-purpose room here provides a useful space for formal entertaining.

OPPOSITE When not in use, the same furniture provides plenty of space in which to work from home.

The Primary Function

The first stage in the planning process of any decorative scheme is to focus on the intended function of the room or open-plan space.

THE MULTIPURPOSE ROOM

By considering all the rooms in your home at the same time – including those that you don't intend to decorate – you might be able to reallocate their functions. Depending on how much space you have, you might want to look at the following additional uses for your rooms.

SITTING ROOM	media room, library
DINING ROOM	media room, home office, playroom, library
KITCHEN	dining room, office, media room, sitting room
CONSERVATORY	dining room, playroom, home office
BEDROOM	media room, home office, library
SPARE BEDROOM	dressing room, home office
HALL OR LANDING	library, additional storage

ANSWER THESE QUESTIONS

* What are you intending the primary function of the room to be? Try to think beyond the established use of individual rooms. For example, if you live on a road with a great deal of traffic noise, would it be best to have the bedrooms at the back of the property and then to use any rooms at the front as a spare room, dressing room or bathroom? Or if you have a ground-floor living room with little natural light, would it be better to move the main living room to the first floor instead? For the best possible use of space it is essential that you think laterally.

* In addition to the room's primary function (such as cooking, eating, relaxing, studying, sleeping or bathing) will the space have any secondary function?

* In order for a room to fulfill its primary function or combined functions what furniture and lighting will you need to accommodate?

* If the room is to have a secondary function how will it be structured? Will you need to provide special lighting and storage?

The Basic Ingredients

Once you have decided on the function of your room,
it's now time to focus on the ingredients needed to achieve it.

Always write a detailed list of the main elements required in a room before you start the process of deciding on its visual appearence and then try to adhere to these requirements as closely as possible. The reason for this is that during the planning process you will be faced with thousands of different options and it is easy to be swayed by style rather than the practical essentials. For example, during the early stages of the planning process you might decide that a room will have a durable, warm, low-maintenance surface because it will be used as a playroom. Later on in the process, having been influenced by a visit to a flooring showroom, you might feel that the style that you want to achieve calls for oak floorboards rather than anything as apparently prosaic as linoleum. Or when choosing suitable storage for a sitting room you might fall in love with a beautiful French armoire, when in fact you really need built-in storage that will accommodate the complex wiring required for a home entertainment system.

CONSIDER EACH INGREDIENT IN YOUR ROOM
* **Electrics** Decide where the electrical sockets and lighting should go.
* **Heating** If you are reorganizing the layout you may have to move radiators.
* **Flooring** If there is heavy foot traffic you may want to consider a robust floorcovering.
* **Storage** Decide which items you will have to store and which can be kept elsewhere.
* **Furniture** Consider which items of furniture are necessary for the function of the room.

ABOVE Before: the only item that had to be incorporated was a Regency-style sofa.
LEFT After: the sofa sets the tone for the scheme of the window treatments and furniture.

OPPOSITE (BELOW) The bathroom before decoration.
OPPOSITE (ABOVE) After: the bathroom space has been maximized, allowing room for twin sinks with storage below.

WORKING WITH WHAT YOU HAVE

There's no doubt that the easiest decorating projects are those that start with a blank canvas. However, most of us, for reasons of economy or sentimentality, have existing items of furniture, lighting and pictures that have to be incorporated into a new scheme. The extent to which these will dominate your room will depend on their size and style.

When planning the contents of a room that you are decorating, write an inventory of the other items of furniture in your home – do this even if you are only planning to decorate one room. With a heading for each room write a list of all the large pieces of furniture and take a view on which pieces are best suited to which rooms. Remember that as your scheme takes shape items in other rooms can be painted or reupholstered so that they can be integrated compatibly to suit the look.

THIS PAGE Even the creation of a
simple scheme will require a great
deal of preparation. Having created
the structure of the room you may
then want to allow the look to evolve.
OPPOSITE When planning a project,
collect pictures of furniture and
samples of any fabrics and wallpaper
that you may like to use.

The Search for Inspiration

With so much choice available, it's worth taking the time to do some thorough research so that you are completely clear about how you want your room to look.

The most enjoyable part of the planning stage is the search for inspiration. Few of us have the creative genius required to summon up an image in our minds of the way that we want a room to look. Instead we have to rely on a variety of different visual sources to inspire our ideas.

When planning a project compile folders of images that you think will be useful. There are a variety of sources that you can plunder: magazines, books, catalogues, brochures or the internet. If a book or magazine is too precious to tear up then make colour photocopies. Don't just look at the obvious sources – something as simple as an image on a postcard can provide an idea for a colour combination.

A tool that will prove useful in this process is a digital camera, which offers an inexpensive and instantaneous way to record anything that sparks off ideas. As you do your research, take photographs of everything that catches your eye, from items of furniture to the tiniest upholstery details. At this stage it is essential that you consider everything you see – you can always discard them at a later stage.

It pays to be scientific in your approach; as you trawl through this material divide your ideas into categories under the following headings: colours, textures, walls, floors, furniture and lighting. As each category grows, the process of defining and refining your ideas will progress.

CHOOSING THE RIGHT STYLE FOR YOUR HOUSE

One way of choosing a style of decoration is to be led by the period of the house. In the 1980s many owners of period homes decorated rooms with their interpretations of the way that the house might have been decorated when it was first built – for example, a house built in the late 18th century would have neo-classical furniture and fabrics, while one built in the late 19th century would be decorated in a Victorian style. While this is now considered by many to be a rather limiting approach, it can make sense to decorate a house in a way that is sympathetic to its architecture and history. For example, decorating a country cottage with low ceilings in the style of a grand Georgian manor house will inevitably produce a confused, rather overbearing look. Instead, consider a style that is true to the spirit of simple rustic interiors but that stops short of being a slavish copy of a period look. Similarly, if you are decorating a Georgian house with high ceilings, you might want to allude to its past with a formal style of furniture and curtains, but update the look by using a pale, neutral palette of colours.

TOOLS OF THE TRADE

* Interior design books, magazines and brochures
* Clear folders with labels in which to collect your ideas
* A digital camera

The Agony of Choice

The next stage is to translate all of your ideas into paint, wallpaper, fabric and furniture.

Anyone who has ever completed a decorating project will tell you that by far the most time-consuming part of the task is not the actual painting or wallpapering but the research – in other words hunting for the paint colours, wallpapers, fabrics and flooring. The problem is that we are, quite literally, spoilt for choice; if you look at a single paint chart you'll see before you row after row of colours in every imaginable hue. The same is true of almost every element of the interior that you set out to find – from the simplest fabric to the most elaborate chandelier – and the more you look, the more choices you'll be offered.

There are times during the early stages of a project when the simple act of choosing the various elements required to create a decorating scheme will seem insurmountable. It is for this reason that once you have completed your research the next step is to focus your disparate thoughts with the help of a moodboard.

CREATING A MOODBOARD

Every decorating project is a journey into the unknown. And however long or short a new journey is, it is essential that we decide exactly where we are going. The purpose of a moodboard is to turn your ideas into reality. One of the most difficult aspects in the early stages of any decorating project is the need to visualize the way that a room will look. The reason that a moodboard is essential is because it is the closest that you will ever get to imagining a proposed scheme without creating a computer-generated image. In many respects it is more effective because it gives you a better idea of how colours and textures will look when they are put together.

A moodboard can take a number of different forms. It can be as simple as a wall-mounted pinboard on which you collect all the samples of paint, fabrics, wallpapers and flooring that you have accumulated during the course of your research, as well as photographs of any items of furniture, lighting and accessories that you might be considering. Alternatively, you might wish to glue or staple all of your samples to a large piece of card. Although this might be a messier, less flexible option, it does have the advantage of being more portable.

The inspiration for your moodboard should be all of the visual material that you have collected together. Start by laying everything out on a table or on the floor and use the images and samples to make the following choices (see the box on the right):

MOODBOARD INSPIRATION

* Would you like the overall style of the room to be classic, contemporary, functional or maybe a combination of these?

* Is there a particular style you want to achieve? Giving the style a name will help you focus on your visual choice. Is it classic English? Liveable modern? Minimalist? Classic French? Casual French? Exotic? If it doesn't fall into an existing description, then make up your own name – maybe a 'modern rustic', 'simple Georgian' or 'Paris apartment'.

* Is there a key word that exemplifies your choice, such as 'clean', 'intimate' or 'formal'?

* Is there a particular colour or combination of colours that you would like to dominate the scheme?

OPPOSITE A moodboard with samples of fabrics, wallpapers, trimmings and inspirational photographs.

RIGHT Always combine samples of preferred fabrics, paints and wallpapers before embarking on a project.
BELOW RIGHT Then, when the project is completed, there'll be no surprises.

WRITING A BRIEF

Use your answers to write your own decorating brief. Imagine that you are commissioning an interior designer, and specify the style and function of the room, and detail which items of furniture you would like to use. The process of articulating what it is that you want to achieve will help you turn your ideas into reality.

Having written your decorating brief, use your moodboard to help you achieve it. While your files of inspirational material will have given you the general ideas about what you want to create, the moodboard is about identifying the specific elements of your scheme.

GATHERING SAMPLES

Your moodboard should be an edited selection of the paint, wallpaper, fabric and furniture that will be used to create your scheme. The more samples that you have to choose from, the better your moodboard – and your final scheme – will be.

Most major fabric manufacturers will give you small samples of fabric known as 'swatches'. In some instances, particularly in the case of fabrics with large-scale patterns, you might want a bigger sample. If the fabric in question is inexpensive, you could consider buying a sample length. Alternatively, most manufacturers will lend you a large sample in return for a deposit that will be refunded when you return it. Most paint and wallpaper manufacturers also offer samples – although in the case of paint there will usually be a small charge.

When selecting paint for a moodboard, apply two or three layers to small pieces of paper or card. It is essential that every sample you add to a board is clearly marked with the name of the manufacturer and the reference.

The other ingredients necessary for a moodboard include samples of flooring and any tassles or trimmings, such as cord or braid, that you might be considering. In the case of samples of flooring that are either too large or unwieldy, use a colour photocopier to give you a visual reference, scaled-down if necessary, of the original. Also include colour photocopies or photographs of key pieces of furniture that are to be integrated into the scheme.

Although the moodboard process might sound time-consuming and fiddly, there is every chance that you'll find it extremely enjoyable. It is an invaluable stage of the decorating schedule – and will give you the best possible chance of creating the ideal scheme.

KEEPING YOUR OPTIONS OPEN

When collecting samples for a moodboard choose fabrics, wallpapers and paints in a variety of colours for each element in the room. A decorator uses a moodboard in a way that is similar to how an artist mixes paint, ensuring that the overall colour is in a constant state of evolution until precisely the right hue has been achieved. A decorator uses a moodboard in the same way, mixing different colours and textures to achieve the right look. Keep your options open by never dismissing samples until you are happy with the scheme; changing one element can create a knock-on effect that requires you to alter other colours within the room. Never throw away samples as they will come in useful when planning other decorating schemes – use them to create your own personal library, making sure that you label each one with the name of the manufacturer, price and the design reference.

CREATING A FLOOR PLAN

As your moodboard takes shape, keep referring back to your original brief and use graph paper create a scale plan of your room that shows the position of windows and doors, as well as proposed and existing power sockets and lighting. Cut out shapes that represent pieces of furniture that you are considering using in the scheme. If a piece of furniture doesn't fit, or seems surplus to requirements, don't even consider it.

REFINING YOUR IDEAS

Use your moodboard, decorating brief and floor plan to write a detailed specification for the room. The specification should outline how you intend to approach each of the following:

Walls

Paintwork

Flooring

Blinds, curtains and shutters

Items of furniture to be included (with details of upholstery)

Flooring

Lighting

THE FINALIZED MOODBOARD

In order to distil your ideas, you should now make a second moodboard that specifies just the fabrics, furniture and paint that you have decided to use. This is the final opportunity to ensure that it all works as a cohesive whole.

3

Colour, Pattern & Texture

Successful decorating is about more than just painting the walls
and choosing curtains – it is about balancing colours, patterns and
textures to create a harmonious feel. If it sounds complicated,
rest assured that there's no real mystery. Instead it relies on
a combination of your own instincts that will tell you what works
and what doesn't work and also on experimentation. You only
need to mix samples of different patterns, textures and colours
to soon recognize what works best for you. You will also discover
that this mixing and matching is one of the most enjoyable stages
in the decorating process.

Choosing Colour

Selecting a colour scheme sets the tone of a room: a historic colour for a period style, bright colours for a nursery, white for a minimal look, calming greens for a bedroom.

When we talk about the colour of a room we tend to mean the walls. Yet while the colour you choose for your walls is important, it is by no means the only way to add colour to a scheme. When planning a project, take a 'holistic' approach to colour; one of the chief reasons why the moodboard described in the last chapter is so important is because it encourages you to think about all of the elements – fabrics, furniture and flooring – at the same time, and in particular to consider their colour.

However colours of these elements is not the only choice to make. Just as important are the qualities that link them, namely pattern and texture. Here, we will see how achieving a balance between the three elements of colour, pattern and texture is the secret to creating the perfect interior scheme.

CREATING COLOUR GROUPS

When considering colour for walls, fabrics, furniture or flooring it can be helpful not to think just in terms of colour categories such as pinks, blues and greens, but also in terms of their tonal qualities. Some colours – pale blues and green for instance – often have much more in common with one another than with the more intense shades of the same colours. There are many ways of categorizing colours, but the following ones can be a useful way of dividing colours into groups.

WHITES AND OFF-WHITES The most successful whites are rarely pure, brilliant whites, because these tend to be too stark, particularly in rooms in which there is a great deal of light. Instead, a white should have some other, almost imperceptible hue that helps to soften it without colouring it. Whites will appear to change visually when used in combination with different colours (and vice versa), so it is essential to compare them with other colours in the planned scheme.

NEUTRALS For many, neutrals offer a softer alternative to whites and off-whites. The term covers a variety of different hues, from creams through to greys and pale browns. Unless you are trying to create a moody, exotic look it is better to avoid neutrals in rooms where there isn't a lot of light.

COOL COLOURS These offer the best means of creating a soft, feminine feel and range from delicate pinks, blues and greens to more vibrant hues such as aquas and lilacs.

ABOVE One of the best ways to create a feeling of light and space is with an all-white interior.

OPPOSITE In a white room a splash of bold colour is guaranteed to create a dramatic effect.

RIGHT For a cohesive feel, accessories should be an integral part of the colour scheme.

BELOW This bathtub has been integrated into the scheme by painting the sides the same colour as the walls.

OPPOSITE A combination of creams, whites and naturals offer the easiest, most cost-effective way to create a harmonious scheme. Paint finishes that have been distressed to make them look old, will stop the overall scheme from appearing too clinical. Always paint furniture so that it conforms to the dominant palette of colours.

ABOVE A striking, bold colour can be offset by a calmer shade to create a surprisingly cohesive decorating scheme in this instance. The mixture of contemporary and classic styles in an interior – however unlikely – is surprisingly successful.

HOT COLOURS Introducing vibrant reds, yellows, blues and greens can be an effective way to add an energetic feel to an interior. If you don't want them to become too dominant, however, then balance the intensity of these colours with cool, reflective whites.

RICH COLOURS These are colours with depth such as browns, aubergines and reds, which are ideal for creating either a masculine or an exotic look. In small rooms with little light they can create a snug, warm atmosphere.

MIXING COLOURS

When choosing colours, balance is key. This is why a moodboard is so integral to the planning process. When trying to combine colours, think beyond simply putting together different shades of the same colour. Combining colours in the same tonal range will produce much more

interesting combinations, such as pale blue and mushroom, or pink and grey. Also bear in mind that contrasts between colours are as critical as combinations that complement one another. Perhaps the most popular approach to using colour is to create a white or neutral backdrop with paint, wallpaper and upholstery and to then add splashes of colour in the form of other pieces of upholstered furniture, curtains and accessories.

USING COLOUR TO CREATE HARMONY

Colour is the tool with which you will pull a scheme together. Many schemes, particularly for living rooms, will necessarily include a variety of different elements. With the help of a couple of colours it is possible to create visual order. However, it is essential to consider every element in a room as part of a colour scheme; the colour of the furniture and flooring is of equal importance as the fabric and wallpaper.

ABOVE In this more traditional scheme, the dark paint colour on the walls has been balanced by the lighter colours of the table linen and upholstery. The colour in the discreetly patterned fabrics co-ordinates with the colour on the walls.

Types of Pattern

In a harmonious scheme even the boldest pattern can be incorporated into a room to create a striking effect. The secret is balance.

THE QUESTION OF SCALE

Many people shy away from using large-scale pattern. There is no doubt that some can be overbearing, particularly those that incorporate three or four different colours, such as an old-fashioned chintz. However, the secret to successfully using large-scale pattern relies on the pattern, colour and scale of other elements in the room – such as other fabrics and wallpapers – and its overall style. For example, a simple scheme in which the dominant colour in a complex print has also been used for the walls can look surprisingly contemporary. An even simpler option is to combine the patterned fabric with pale, neutral colours. Patterns with just two colours, such as red and white, are much easier to use, particularly any that have a 'distressed' appearance.

Another common tendency is to avoid using large-scale patterns in small rooms – this can be a design error, as anything large-scale, whether it is pattern or furniture, tends to make small rooms appear larger rather than smaller. As well as florals, other large-scale patterns include pictorials such as toile de Jouy, graphic pattern and damasks.

Small-scale pattern tends to create a more intimate, delicate feel. Nevertheless, the same rules that apply to incorporating large-scale pattern into a scheme apply to small-scale designs – always ensure that the colours work together.

OPPOSITE In many modern schemes one of the most popular ways to use pattern is to put one bold design against a plain backdrop, as well as to use plains in one or more complementary colours.

RIGHT The easiest patterns to use are those that combine one colour with white. Even bold, large-scale patterns, such as this classic design, can be successfully incorporated into an interior.

BELOW Wherever possible, try to ensure that every element, from tableware to upholstery, is an integral part of the overall scheme. While it isn't essential that patterns and colours match, it is important that they complement one another.

RIGHT Here a combination of florals lend a quirky feel to this fitted bench seat – changing them from time to time is an easy way to quickly and easily change the look.

FLORALS

There are, broadly speaking, three types of floral, all of which are distinct in style and create very different looks. The first type is classic florals, most of which are based on botanical drawings with a detailed, finely drawn appearance. The second category is modern florals that is looser and more 'painterly' in style, and the third is smaller-scale, Victorian-style florals, often depicting simple forms such as rosebuds. In addition there are a growing number of simple, graphic florals with a more contemporary feel.

The key to successfully using florals – just like any other pattern – is either to ensure that the dominant colour works with others in the scheme, or to simply use them to provide a 'splash' of pattern and colour against a neutral backdrop. Don't be afraid to mix styles; just because a fabric is in a classic style doesn't mean that it can only be used in a traditional scheme – far more important than the style is the colour.

LEFT This quirky wallpaper design has been incorporated into the bedroom scheme by mixing it with bed linen and upholstery in similar monochrome colours. Mirrored furniture and glass table lamps create a glamorous feel.

PICTORIAL

Probably the best-known pictorial pattern is toile de Jouy, a classic style based on 18th-century documents that depict bucolic scenes. These patterns have been a popular choice for traditional schemes, particularly bedrooms. There are a variety of other pictorial fabrics, ranging from those based on hunting scenes to architectural prints. Whichever style you choose, it is likely to create a soft, feminine feel with exception of those in a bolder modern pictorial style that create something more quirky and contemporary. Once again, the most important element is colour rather than style.

GEOMETRICS

Bold geometric patterns are currently enjoying a revival. Their heyday was in the 1950s and 1960s when they were a key part of the modernist look that prevailed in the post-war era. In their new incarnation, geometrics have a somewhat more discreet, luxurious feel, thanks to the exciting range of new textures and colours. While they are useful for creating a 'retro' Fifties look, they combine equally well with a variety of different styles, from classic to contemporary.

OPPOSITE Don't be afraid to use bold, large-scale patterns in a small room. If it is part of a cohesive scheme, such as this black and white bathroom, it won't be too overpowering.

ABOVE Increasingly, pattern is being used within contemporary schemes; this simple, graphic pattern co-ordinates perfectly with the kitchen cabinets and the floor rug.

OPPOSITE A combination of just one striking pattern with accessories in complementary colours can transform an interior. When the backdrop is plain and minimal, the result has even more impact.

BELOW A variety of discreet patterns in complementary colours has been used to create a cohesive scheme. The silk cushions add a luxurious feel.

STRIPES AND CHECKS

These are a staple of decorating and traditionally used as part of classic English, French and Swedish schemes. Much of their appeal is that they mix well with florals, particularly when in combination with plain colours. Their simplicity also means that they work equally well in more contemporary schemes. Another advantage of basic checks and stripes is that they tend to be available at reasonable prices. The fact that many started off life as utility fabrics – ticking being the most obvious example – means that prices have always been quite modest.

MIXING PATTERN

This is often regarded as the most difficult task that faces anyone planning a decorating project. But, as with so many aspects of decorating, it is made much easier with the help of a moodboard, which makes it clear from the outset what will – and won't – work. As discussed elsewhere in this chapter, the contemporary approach to pattern is to use just one patterned element in an otherwise plain scheme. In the past, many decorators were more adventurous when mixing a variety of patterns – perhaps two or three types of floral plus a few plains and some small-scale geometric design. There is also, of course, a midway point between these two extremes. One option is the classic mixture of floral, plain and check, but it is possible to create variations on this theme, perhaps substituting a stripe for a check, or a geometric for a floral. The basic rules remain the same – colour, scale and texture are all. An increasingly popular way to mix pattern is by combining a plain and patterned fabric on the same chair, sofa or curtain. Not only does this help achieve a quirky feel but it also allows you to incorporate more expensive fabrics that you might not otherwise have been able to afford. Similarly, just one wall hung with a patterned wallpaper with others painted in a complementary colour allows you to use bold pattern without it becoming overbearing.

Texture

Textures offer visual and tactile qualities that are essential to every scheme, particularly those that are contemporary in style.

While colour and pattern tend to get a great deal of attention, texture often gets overlooked. However it cannot be ignored in interior design – it is an integral part of fabrics, paint, wallcoverings, furniture and flooring. Texture gives a material an extra dimension that in some cases is as important than colour, and in many instances it will have a significant influence on the way that a colour appears. Textural ingredients are particularly relevant to clean, contemporary interiors; in the absence of pattern, texture becomes vital in creating a layered, luxurious feel that is an essential feature of both bedrooms and living rooms.

SHINY

Glossy surfaces on fabrics, walls, furniture or flooring have always been a valued element in interior design. Before the advent of electric lighting, it was a quality that was particularly important because it made the most of any available light. Today, the integration of glossy features has more relevance to creating a vibrant, glamorous interior. Silk, viscose and rayon all have light-reflective qualities, but also don't overlook the growing number of reflective, metallic-effect wallpapers. Furniture and flooring with a high-gloss finish all create a similar effect – consider lacquer, glazed terracotta and highly polished or varnished wood.

ABOVE A combination of a matt and a shiny finish give a glamorous, contemporary feel to this period room.
LEFT Woven fabrics are not only luxurious to touch, but often have a lustre that makes them look great, too.
OPPOSITE A combination of mirrored surfaces, Perspex and lustrous fabrics create a striking feel in this bedroom.

ROUGH

Surfaces that are rough to the touch, such as contemporary structured weaves, linen, stone floors or wood, don't just look good – they feel good, too. It is for this reason that when choosing elements for a scheme you should always touch them and not just rely on the visual impression.

COMBINING TEXTURES

Like mixing pattern and colour, combining textures is all about putting together elements that don't just complement each other but also provide a contrast. A good example is pairing linen and velvet; one has a rough, flat, almost rustic feel while the other has a deep-piled soft texture and lustrous quality. In the same way that mixing one colour with another can enhance it, so too can mixing textures. Next to linen, velvet seems even more indulgent and next to velvet, linen seems more rough and satisfying. It is for these reasons that backing a throw with velvet or simply adding a velvet ribbon to the edge of a curtain or blind can create a wonderful sophisticated look.

OPPOSITE The combination of these fabrics, flooring and accessories would add texture and warmth to an interior.
BELOW LEFT This distressed wall finish has far more depth of colour than a plain paint. The chair is upholstered in a patchwork of textured fabrics.
BELOW RIGHT This striking pairing of contemporary fabrics illustrates how texture can lend a luxurious look to a piece of furniture.

4

Wallcoverings

When deciding how to decorate the walls of a room, the choice is so vast that it is small wonder that so many people opt for a finish as inoffensive as cream or magnolia. There's nothing wrong with either of these colours, particularly if you want to create a neutral backdrop, but there are many other creative options if you want the walls to be a fundamental part of your scheme. Decorating walls doesn't need to be confined to paint and wallpaper, so consider the whole range of options from the unobtrusive style of panelling to the vibrant feel of a bold wallpaper. Whichever you decide on, ensure that your choice is an integral part of the whole scheme rather than a dominant feature – balance is all.

Decorating Options for Walls

When choosing colours and textures for walls the possibilities are seemingly infinite – from paint in almost every imaginable hue to patterned wallpapers and finishes.

While there is no doubt that wall treatments are a key part of a scheme, their role should be kept in proportion to other elements; such as flooring and upholstery so that they form an integral part of the look that you are putting together. The invaluable contribution of a moodboard is because it encourages you to create a balance between these three elements and doesn't allow any treatment of the walls to dominate.

PAINT

As well as providing the quickest, easiest and most cost-effective way to decorate walls, paint also offers a huge choice. The shade you choose will be governed by many things: the colour of different elements in the room, for example, as well as the prevailing style that you wish to create. It will also be governed by your intuition – and any conscious and subconscious associations you may have. Yet colour is rarely static and it is important to study how a particular hue will respond to the changing light in a room; the shade you see on a paint chart will differ enormously from a sample colour painted on a patch of wall seen in the early morning. And, because of the way that the light changes during the course of the day that colour will evolve constantly, and again in the evening when it is subjected to artificial light. For this reason you should set aside plenty of time for experimentation and constantly monitor changes throughout the day. The advantage of using a moodboard is that you don't then have to abide by any particular rules; it's simply a case of what works on a moodboard will work in your scheme.

One often-quoted rule is that light colours will make a room look larger than one painted in dark colours. This is sometimes the case, but the reality is considerably more complex than this because the way that we perceive the size of a room depends on a variety of other factors, including the amount of natural light as well as the scale and quantity of the furniture. Many darker colours – dark browns, reds and mossy greens, for example – often have considerably more depth than their lighter relations and this helps to blur the boundaries of space. So don't immediately gravitate to the lighter colours on a paint chart simply because you feel that they will enhance the feeling of space.

Remember, too, that paint can have its limitations; conventional paint applied with a brush or roller will only ever offer a flat surface. There are, of course, exceptions – wonderful textured, chalky paints and paint finishes that help to add an additional dimension to a wall.

OPPOSITE AND ABOVE Choosing sympathetic colours for walls and paintwork that add a deep, lustrous feel will create a look so pleasing that little more decoration is necessary. In some cases a striking piece of furniture or accessory is all that is required.

Whichever colour or texture you choose, the best schemes are most likely to be those in which the walls simply form a backdrop, rather than offering the main attraction. However tempting it may be to make a bold statement with a vivid colour, a more cohesive solution creates a calm and well-integrated scheme.

PAINT EFFECTS AND STENCILS

The fact that paint effects, like so many other decorative elements, became so elaborate and overdone in the 1980s doesn't mean they aren't a useful addition to a scheme or should be ignored. Used in moderation, paint finishes such as ragging and dragging offer the appearance, rather than the feel, of texture. They are particularly effective in rooms that have large expanses of featureless wall.

Elaborate stencils are another decorative element that can dominate a scheme. In their modern incarnation, stencils tend to consist of simple, graphic patterns in just one or two colours.

When putting together a moodboard create samples of the different effects, designs and colours that you are considering and add them to the scheme in the same way that you would a fabric or wallpaper.

ABOVE A subtle paint finish provides the perfect complementary backdrop to this classic Swedish clock.

LEFT Here, a trailing two-colour design offers a restrained scheme for hall, stairs and landing.

OPPOSITE Mixed with sympathetic vintage furniture, fabrics and accessories this simple stencilled design in a mixture of aubergine and white creates a discreet yet decorative backdrop to this simple scheme.

WALLPAPER

There are two reasons why many people who are planning a decorating project shy away from the idea of using wallpaper: one is that choosing and integrating pattern is more difficult than selecting a paint colour, and the other is because it seems comparatively more difficult to hang. While there is a certain amount of truth in these beliefs, they are counterbalanced by two equally convincing arguments in favour of wallpaper: it provides a wonderful finish that is much more durable than paint, and when it is patterned it offers a simple and easy way to decorate a room, doing away with the need for much additional decorative interest.

The other advantage of wallpaper is that it offers a huge variety of possibilities that go far beyond just patterned designs – it can also provide a way of integrating further visual stimulation, ranging from wonderful rough textures to shiny metallics.

ABOVE The discreet pattern on the wall behind these simple shelves creates an unobtrusive backdrop to a collection of contemporary ceramics. **LEFT** Many wallpapers offer a quick and convenient way to add textures that would otherwise require costly, highly-skilled workmanship. **OPPOSITE** This quirky two-coloured wallpaper has been mixed with a Perspex console table, silver accessories and a Venetian-style mirror to create a striking look that is a perfect blend of new and old.

The way in which wallpaper is used has changed in recent years. The classic approach is to hang it on all the walls in a room. In the case of large-scale patterns, however, the effect of this can be overpowering. In contemporary schemes a striking wallpaper design is used on just one wall while the remaining walls are painted in a complementary colour.

However don't be afraid to use wallpaper with large patterns on all four walls, even in small rooms; when offset by plain fabrics and flooring they offer a good way to create a striking scheme.

FABRIC-LINED WALLS

This traditional option offers a device for creating a cosy environment that is ideal for bedrooms and dressing rooms. The technique involves stretching battens on walls so, unless you are intending to use it extensively throughout the house, it might be a job best left to a professional. (Bear in mind that generally the cost is likely to be considerably higher than for hanging wallpaper.) One advantage of using fabric on walls is that it allows you to use designs and create patterns and that feature on a much larger scale than most wallpapers.

ABOVE When choosing a distinctive pattern, create a striking look by combining it with complementary accessories that play on the same colour combinations.

LEFT A good example of how the pairing of a classic pattern with a subtle colour can be used to create a discreet backdrop to an interior.

OPPOSITE Mixing bold or richly coloured wallpaper with plain paintwork can create a more restrained feel than hanging the same wallpaper design on all four walls.

ABOVE Here, wooden panels have been applied to the wall, adding interest and helping to manipulate the proportions of the room. It is a great option for dull or featureless areas of wall.

PANELLING

This is one of the key ingredients in classic decoration. However, in the past, panelling had a practical function, helping to insulate rooms against damp and draughts. Today, the purpose of panelling is purely aesthetic, offering a way of giving a feeling of intimacy to a room. It can also effectively manipulate the proportions of an interior, for example in a room with low ceilings where the addition of panelling that reaches a third of the way up the wall will make the ceiling seem higher. Panelling also offers a good way to add interest to otherwise dull, featureless walls.

In its most elaborate form, panelling is expensive to fit, especially when hardwoods are used. However, there are plenty of simpler alternatives available that mimic the effect of authentic panelling for a fraction of the cost of the real thing. Another option is tongue-and-groove panelling – this is formed of interlocking planks of wood that are fixed vertically to walls. Again, there is a much simpler alternative, which involves fixing sheets of MDF that are machined to look like tongue-and-groove panelling. Increasingly, many contemporary designers now use sheets of thin ply screwed to walls to add decorative interest.

ABOVE Squares of plywood add texture and colour to one of the walls in this bathroom. The direction of the grain in the wood has been arranged so that none of the neighbouring squares follow the same direction.

TILES

For centuries ceramic tiles have been used to protect walls in bathrooms and kitchens from water, and to create an easily cleaned surface. Today there are a number of other alternatives that fulfil these requirements – these include special waterproof finishes as well as the use of materials such as glass and stainless steel. The more conventional option of ceramic tiles, however, offers an excellent way of creating a specific visual style, such as rustic, mediterranean or Victorian, using tiles that reflect those styles.

OPPOSITE Tiles have been used to create a dramatic, chequerboard pattern on both walls and floors. **BELOW** Mosaic tiles create a striking impression and are much easier to fit than you might imagine since they come in webbing-backed sheets.

MIRROR

This inexpensive, yet highly effective, wallcovering is often overlooked as a wall treatment. The main attraction is that using mirrored surfaces offers a way of creating a spacious feel within even the smallest room because it appears to break down rigid wall barriers, allowing you to look beyond them. Be aware, however, that covering large areas of wall with mirrors can be disconcerting because you lose your physical awareness of the perimeters of the room; as a result, mirrors often look best when they are fitted into alcoves or just to one wall.

MIXING WALL TREATMENTS

You may find that your interior will benefit from a combination of different wall treatments. While it should be recognized that combining too many different materials might make a room look fussy, a careful juxtaposition, such as panelling that reaches halfway up the wall combined with a striking wallpaper can create a simple, pleasing look.

OPPOSITE In this bathroom a framed mirror has been applied to the wall and succeeds in creating the impression of additional space.

BELOW LEFT A striking black-and-white wallpaper has been used to create three horizontal panels behind a bed. This is an inexpensive way to create a luxurious look.

BELOW RIGHT Consider using paint beneath the dado rail and patterned wallpaper above. Here, a deep moulding is a contemporary take on a traditional architectural detail.

5

Flooring

Flooring is as important a part of the overall scheme as paint or fabric. Making sure that it works with the other elements in the interior will guarantee you achieve a harmonious look.

Because flooring tends to be one of the more expensive elements in a scheme, it is critical to get it right. While practicality is a key consideration, so too are aesthetics. For this reason, consider the colour and texture of flooring in the same way that you would the colour and texture of a fabric, paint or wallpaper. The type of flooring you choose should be governed by the function of the room – for instance, a hallway that has a great deal of traffic will require a far more hard-wearing floor than a spare bedroom. The other single most important practical consideration is cleaning – so while some wonderful textured terracotta floor might look great as part of a scheme for a kitchen, think long and hard about how easy it will be to clean regularly.

Carpet

Comfort or practicality? This is the issue with carpets – unsuitable for wet shoes and heavy use, but providing warmth and a welcoming softness underfoot.

There is no doubt that fitted wall-to-wall carpets are the most comfortable option – sadly there is also no doubt that they are not especially practical. The answer is to think very carefully about where a carpet will provide a functional and desirable option (for example, in a bedroom or a cold room) and to choose other types of flooring when it won't.

CHOOSING A CARPET

Before you think about texture, consider the colour. On the whole, light-coloured carpets will make a room look bigger, but very light carpets will highlight any dirt. The best colours are mid-tone, such as beige, taupe, grey or pale brown. In living rooms interior designers work on the basis that a carpet should be a few tones darker than the upholstery. In a bedroom, you may decide that because of the low traffic, you can treat yourself to a pale colour that will create a light, airy mood. When choosing a bold 'statement' colour, ensure that it works as part of the scheme in the same way as paint or soft furnishings. In a hall, practicality has to be the priority so a dark carpet, ideally one that is 80 per cent wool and 20 per cent nylon, will be the most sensible option. Never lay carpets in kitchens or bathrooms.

ABOVE A striped stair runner in subtle colours co-ordinates with the other elements in the scheme.
LEFT Two tones of the same carpet have been used to create a stunning broad stripe which, like panelling, can be used to manipulate the proportions of a room.
OPPOSITE For schemes with a contemporary feel, choose a rug with a large-scale, graphic pattern.

TYPES OF CARPET

Carpet can be made in two different ways and is described as either woven or tufted. The most durable carpets are those that are woven (they are also the most expensive). The two most popular types of woven carpet are Axminster, which is available in a variety of decorative patterns, and Wilton, which is only made in five different colours. Tufted carpets are made with tufts inserted through holes in the backing.

VELVET This is a cut-pile carpet with a smooth, uniform appearance that is best suited to areas of low traffic.

TWIST Similar to velvet, this carpet has slightly twisted fibres which give it an uneven surface. This quality makes it easier to maintain and more durable than velvet.

LOOP PILE This increasingly popular style of carpet is the carpet industry's answer to natural flooring such as sisal and coir. Their looped construction gives them a visually appealing texture and makes them extremely hard-wearing.

SAXONY A luxurious, deep-pile option that is best for areas of low traffic as the pile tends to flatten.

SHAG PILE The fibres in this style of carpet tend to be around 15mm (½in) long. Like Saxony, it will flatten with time.

MAINTENANCE

One of the best ways to ensure that a carpet keeps its looks is make sure that it has been treated with Scotchguard (it is advisable to have this done during manufacture rather that once it has been laid). Carpets will also have a far longer life and require less maintenance if they are not subjected to outdoor shoes.

SISAL, SEAGRASS AND COIR

This type of rough-textured natural flooring offers a combination of the relaxed feel of wooden floors with some of the comfort of carpet. However, it usually won't have the durability of either, and stain removal can be problematic. A good-quality underlay will do a great deal to ensure that a natural flooring will have the longest possible life. In the carpet trade, opinion is split over whether these materials are suitable for stairs.

OPPOSITE Natural flooring such as sisal, seagrass and coir is a practical option that will add texture to both contemporary and traditional interiors.

Wood

Wooden floors might create a sleek, luxurious look but in some rooms their advantages outweigh their pitfalls. A combination of wood and carpet offers the best of both worlds.

Wooden floors come in a huge variety of guises, from the simplest, most inexpensive option of painted floorboards to the ultimate luxury of polished hardwood such as oak or cherry. There are plenty of choices in between, including parquet and low-cost laminates. While wood is undoubtedly the most visually appealing flooring option, offering a combination of texture and rich natural colour, unless it is covered with rugs or runners it is much noisier than carpet (in apartment buildings, consider the impact of wooden floors on your neighbours). It is also not the ideal option for children, particularly when they are crawling or playing. Before choosing wood look at its colour as part of the overall scheme and make sure that it works well in combination with the paint colours and upholstery you have chosen.

OPPOSITE (ABOVE) Either real or simulated wood adds texture and colour to an interior.
OPPOSITE (BELOW) Painting a floor white will create a light, airy feel in any room.
THIS PAGE A highly polished wooden floor creates a striking look in this kitchen-dining room.

Ceramic Tiles

For centuries, terracotta has offered inexpensive, easily maintained flooring. Today, it is part of both traditional and classic interiors that combine good looks with practicality.

OPPOSITE A combination of terracotta tiles and a striped cotton rug mix comfort with practicality in this simple, rustic bedroom.

LEFT In this kitchen a ceramic floor creates an airy, contemporary feel. The only disadvantage of ceramic floors in a kitchen is that they are less forgiving when breakables are dropped.

For areas that are subjected to heavy traffic, dirt and water, a ceramic floor is a good option. For this reason it is an ideal choice for halls, kitchens and bathrooms. However, do bear in mind that any items dropped on a tiled floor are likely to break immediately on impact.

Some of the most practical ceramic tiles are made of smooth, Continental-style porcelain. Vitrified tiles are those that don't require sealing; non-vitrified tiles will have to be sealed before they come into contact with water. Bear in mind that tiles with an uneven, rustic finish aren't the easiest surfaces to keep clean when combined with cement grouting. In addition to conventional terracotta tiles, also consider mosaic tiling that has a luxurious, contemporary feel.

Stone

Whether you want a look that is classic or cutting-edge contemporary, stone offers a huge array of luxurious options. But like ceramic floors they also have hidden pitfalls.

Stone serves a similar purpose to terracotta, but is more expensive and can be trickier to lay. The three most popular types of stone flooring are sandstone, slate and limestone. Most of these are available in a wide variety of different textures, from shiny smooth options with a sleek, contemporary look, to rough and textured finishes that are perfect for creating a rustic feel. If you want to achieve period character you can buy flagstones reclaimed from old buildings. Before making your selection, look at other types of stone, such as marble and travertine – a close relative of limestone – as well as composite stones, made by mixing ground-up stone with a bonding agent. Stone floors can be hard to clean and will cause dropped crockery and glass to break. All porous stone floors should be sealed before use. Also, take the position of the floor into account – on upper floors a strong sub-floor will be required.

OPPOSITE Large squares of stone flooring are the ideal option for cool, contemporary-style interiors.
BELOW This slate floor lends a striking look to this traditional kitchen. Granite work surfaces help to create a cohesive style.

Vinyl & Linoleum

As well as being extremely practical, vinyl and linoleum also provide a dazzling range of colours and decorative choices.

For value for money and a huge range of choice, vinyl and linoleum offer the perfect solution. The two are often confused: vinyl is a purely synthetic product, while linoleum is made from a mixture of linseed-oil and wood flour pressed onto a hessian backing. Linoleum – or lino as it is more commonly known – has a slightly marbled appearance and comes in an almost limitless range of colours that can be mixed to create complex patterns. As a natural product it will age beautifully and will also outlive many synthetic equivalents. At its most basic, vinyl is a utilitarian product with a relatively short life span. However, more sophisticated vinyls are now available that mimic the pattern, colour and texture of natural materials such as wood and stone.

ABOVE Black and white vinyl or linoleum can create a striking, practical floor in bathrooms, kitchens and hallways. To soften the contrast, use a softer alternative to white.

Metal, Rubber, Glass & Cork

When choosing a floor consider the many offbeat options that can be used to create a stylish but practical look in bathrooms and kitchens.

There are a growing number of esoteric options which are well suited to contemporary interiors. Rubber not only has a sleek look, but is also enormously practical and easy to clean, making it perfect for kitchens and nurseries. Metal or reinforced glass flooring is a good choice for a contemporary, utilitarian feel. In recent years cork tiles – especially those printed with photographic images – have become popular.

MIXING FLOORING

Because floors in any home have to accommodate different activities it is a good idea to take a flexible approach. However, be aware that laying different types of flooring in neighbouring rooms can look disjointed when they are seen together – for example, the combination of a wooden floor in a hall, a runner on the stairs and a carpet in the sitting room. An increasingly popular option is to lay wooden floors and to combine them with rugs – a solution that offers the best of both worlds.

ABOVE In this en-suite bathroom rubber creates a practical, stylish floorcovering, with the textured design creating a hard-wearing non-slip surface. In open-plan spaces, different types of flooring help to 'zone' areas such as bathrooms and dining spaces.
LEFT In this bedroom the combination of shiny and matt tiles creates a subtle but striking look.

6

Fabric & Upholstery

A successful combination of fabrics is the secret to achieving the perfect scheme. But, as with every aspect of decorating, plenty of planning and experimentation is required in order to achieve this.

If you think a paint chart offers too much choice then just spend a day trying to choose a fabric. Not only do fabrics come in a huge array of colours, they also offer a seemingly infinite selection of patterns and textures to choose from – plains, stripes, pictorial, geometrics, large and small florals, cottons, woollens are just a few examples. What's more, the products available are constantly expanding, as many major fabric companies add new collections twice a year, thereby offering more and more choice.

Choosing Fabric

Fabrics offer an opportunity to add pattern, colour and teture to a room. Creating the right combination can transform both individual items of furniture and entire schemes.

By the time you start searching for actual fabrics you should have some idea of the look you want to achieve in order to focus your search. Find inspiration by looking at photographs of different types and styles of fabric; even if your decision is as vague as a 'floral' or a 'graphic' it will help you to target your research. It is advisable to visit the fabric manufacturer's showroom rather than a fabric retailer as this will give you the opportunity to see an entire range, rather than an edited selection. To save yourself a repeat visit, collect as many different samples as possible (you will either be able to take these away or they will be sent to you later). Not all showrooms will sell you fabrics direct and might instead refer you to your nearest stockist. To help you in your decision-making process, most manufacturers will also lend you a larger returnable sample on receipt of a small deposit.

One of the reasons that it is important to look at large samples of fabrics is because they give you a better idea of how they feel and how they hang than a smaller sample, so a lightweight cotton will have a very different feel to a heavy wool. Heavier fabrics tend to hang in a more elegant manner and have better insulating properties. In some cases they may be so heavy (when made of wool or tapestry, for example) that they won't need a lining. Medium to lightweight fabrics are better suited to more elaborate window treatments such as swags and tails.

The weight of the fabric you choose for curtains will not only affect the way that they hang but also the amount of light that they allow into a room. When choosing a fabric for upholstery, drape it over furniture to see how it falls. In the case of fabric for both upholstery and curtains, always look at it in all lights.

When buying fabric for upholstery, check that it is robust enough for everyday use. A fabric with a rub test of 25,000 is suitable for general domestic use and one with a rub test of 40,000 is suitable for commercial use. Other points to consider are whether it conforms to safety standards, whether it is washable (and if it is likely to shrink) and whether it is likely to fade in bright sunlight.

OPPOSITE Simple seat covers with frills offer a simple way to add pattern and colour to a scheme. Using two contrasting fabrics when making curtains creates a smart look.

BELOW A loose cover will transform almost any item of upholstered furniture so that it becomes integrated into a scheme. When choosing fabric for a piece of furniture consider how often it will be used; items such as an armchair that are only used occasionally can be covered in a light, plain fabric.

If covering chairs and sofas, patterns tend to be a more sympathetic choice than plain fabrics because they hide creases or marks, whereas plain fabrics tend to show every crease and blemish.

READING THE LABEL

The label on a fabric sample may offer two or three items of information, including the width, the repeat and sometimes the rub test. The standard width of a fabric is 137cm (54in), although it is possible to buy extra-wide fabric measuring up to 300cm (118in) wide. The latter is ideal for making seamless curtains and bedcovers. The repeat refers to the depth of the full pattern on a fabric and is important when estimating quantities. The rub test is the result of a test that gives an indication of how suitable a fabric is for upholstery. Fabric that withstands 20,000 rubs is suitable for light domestic use.

MEASURING UP FOR CURTAINS

Start by measuring the width of the window, taking into account how far the track or pole juts out on either side. The wider the window, the longer the projection should be. Next, multiply the width by 2.25 for fullness, or 1.5 if you're planning to have tab-top eyelet headings, and add allowances for side hems and joining widths. Divide this measurement by the width of your fabric to calculate how many widths are required

ABOVE This luxurious fabric combines luxurious texture with a subtle fringe - it is the perfect option for curtains with a theatrical feel in a formal dining room or living room.

LEFT A floral fabric lined with a bold check creates a striking look that is ideal for a country-style kitchen.

OPPOSITE A simple slip cover can be used to transform a dining room chair.

and then round up the final figure to the next full width. Measure the desired finished length of your curtains and add a minimum of 25cm (10in) for hem allowance and turnings at the top of the curtains (if the fabric is patterned, add the depth of the pattern repeat to the drop). Finally multiply the number of widths by the length, plus allowances, to give you the total number of metres (or feet) required.

CREWELWORK

A plain background fabric is decorated with a chain-stitch design. Crewelwork consisting of multicoloured stitching against a cream or white ground is a key part of traditional English country decorating. There are, however, a growing number of simpler, two-colour crewelwork designs that are ideal for creating a more sophisticated, contemporary look.

LIGHT COTTONS

Cotton fabrics come in a variety of different guises, ranging from lightweight fabrics to heavy canvases and denims. Because they are not as durable or capable of insulation against heat or sunlight, light cottons have only a limited use as furnishing fabrics. However in many traditional schemes cotton florals called chintzes, with a reflective, glazed finish are used for cushions and curtains.

HEAVY COTTONS

Heavy cottons offer a less expensive alternative to wool and linen. Many come in simple stripes such as ticking that started life as a covering for mattresses. They are a durable, functional option for both curtains and upholstery.

DAMASK

This classic fabric can be made of silk, wool, linen, cotton or synthetic fibres and has a pattern woven into it, usually of flowers, fruit or animals.

LINEN

This fabric has experienced a revival of popularity in recent years. Much of its attraction is the wonderful texture that gives it a tactile quality and the fact that with time it takes on a relaxed, informal look that is the antithesis of the tailored style of heavy woollen textiles. This textured quality also makes it a perfect choice for plain schemes as it prevents them from seeming too austere. Another reason for linen's appeal is the way that it holds colour – when dyed, it takes on either a pale, pastel character or heavy, saturated appearance that is perfect for deep browns and reds. Many decorators prefer to use plain linen, but it can look effective when printed with a simple, graphic pattern or with florals against a yellow, 'tea-stained' background.

LINING FABRICS

Curtains and blinds should have a lining that faces the window. Lining tends to be made from plain, off-white fabrics but in some classic schemes curtains are lined with fabric that has a subtle, graphic pattern.

SILK

With its luxurious associations and soft sheen, silk offers the opportunity to add a glamorous touch to an interior. Compared with cotton and linen silk is relatively delicate, but it is ideal for items such as curtains, blinds and accessories that don't get much wear and tear.

Silk is comparatively expensive. However, along with other pricey fabrics such as velvet and high-quality linen, it can be used for smaller items such as stools, curtains and bolsters that will lend the scheme a discreetly luxurious look.

VELVET, CHENILLE, CUT VELVET AND FLOCK

If you're after texture that is soft to the touch, silk or cotton velvet is the ideal choice, although expensive, option. However, as with any good-quality fabric, a little will go a long way – for example a pair of velvet cushions will transform a sofa.

Chenille has a similar quality, although without the wonderful texture, and is a good deal less expensive. Both flock and cut velvet combine a raised decorative design with plain fabric.

VOILE, ORGANZA AND MUSLIN (CHEESECLOTH)

Used as curtains or blinds, these lightweight, semi-transparent fabrics create privacy while also allowing light into a room. Voile curtains are, however, no substitute for those made from cotton, linen and wool drapes. Some interior decorators combine these lightweight fabrics with conventional curtains to provide two different options. Most semi-transparent fabrics are plain, although some are available with a discreet pattern.

WOOL

If it is texture and durability you're after, wool is the best fabric. Its weight makes it perfect for upholstery and, despite being relatively heavy, it can make wonderful curtains that drape elegantly and have excellent insulation properties.

ABOVE LEFT This matching striped blind and cushion have transformed the traditional window seat.
LEFT Box-pleat curtains have a smart, tailored look that is perfect for an elegant bedroom.

THIS PAGE Simple, semi-transparent curtains will create privacy without throwing a room into darkness. Ideally they should be combined with conventional curtains.

Upholstery and Window Treatments

The beauty of upholstered furniture and curtains lies in a combination of carefully chosen fabrics and subtle detailing that adds a tailored, luxurious feel.

Having chosen the fabric, you need to find the loose and fitted covers, curtains, blinds and pelmets that suit the style of your scheme. Here, clever details can make all the difference – a strip of braid running down the length of a curtain, or box pleats that run around an armchair base. Because virtually anything is possible, you should try to do a huge amount of visual research, or refer back to ideas collected earlier.

SOFAS AND CHAIRS

When planning upholstery you need to choose between a fitted or unfitted look. Fitted upholstery is 'close covered', meaning it can't be removed from the main body of the chair or sofa (it can, however, be slipped off seat pads and backs). Loose covers are designed to fit over the piece of furniture and can easily be removed for washing. While unfitted upholstery has practical advantages it does have a much more relaxed look and the fabric will crease more easily. Fitted upholstery will have a tighter, formal appearance.

HEADBOARDS AND VALANCES

The combination of an upholstered headboard and a co-ordinating valance creates a luxurious look in a bedroom, particularly when textured linen or a deep-pile velvet are used. For a clean, contemporary look, choose a tailored rather than a pleated valance.

CURTAINS

The style of curtains can have as much impact on the room as the colour and pattern of the fabric. Designs range from those with discreet details to elaborate arrangements of swags. Even the simplest curtain headings, such as boxed or pinch pleats, can create a superb tailored feel. The best headings are those that stand sufficiently proud to hide the curtain track. More complex treatments based on 18th- and 19th-century styles are making

OPPOSITE Embroidered fabrics and a fringed border on the curtain have been used to lend a decorative touch to this otherwise neutral scheme.
RIGHT Combine textures, colours and patterns in complementary colours to create a layered look.

a comeback, but if you don't want the look to become too overbearing choose plain fabrics or those with a subtle surface texture, such as silk or damask. The type of fabric that you choose will have an impact on the way the curtains hang, so it is important to experiment. Using borders or braid as edging is a great way to add interest to plain, inexpensive curtains. For a classic feel, consider elaborate curtain poles with decorative finials.

BLINDS

Blinds provide a more discreet option to curtains but they don't offer the same insulation to light, noise, heat and cold (although blackout lining will solve this). There are many designs for fabric blinds – the most practical, all-purpose ones are Roman blinds, which draw up into a series of broad, flat folds with rods secured horizontally within pockets. Braid and borders can also be used here to create a discreetly decorative look.

PELMETS

Fabric-covered pelmets are an inexpensive way to create a smart, tailored look and have the advantage of hiding curtain tracks. Consider a design with a shaped profile and also possibly add definition with braid.

THIS PAGE In this neutral scheme a vibrant two-coloured floral has been used to make fabric borders and cushions, and to upholster an ottoman, adding a dramatic splash of pattern and colour.
BELOW LEFT For chairs covered in floral fabrics, consider a rectangular cushion in a complementary colour.

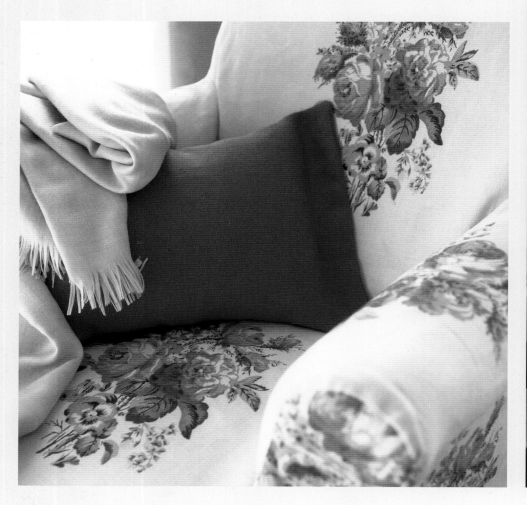

7

Room Solutions

It never pays to make hard-and-fast maxims about decorating. The reason for this is because, in any creative pursuit, rules just cry out to be broken. Additionally, every room requires a different set of rules. Roller blinds might be the best solution for awkwardly shaped windows in a living room, but wouldn't be suitable in a bedroom that faces a busy road lit by street lamps. Terracotta tiles might offer a practical solution for a hallway, but in a kitchen a better option could be a surface such as lino or vinyl that will reduce breakages from dropped glass or crockery. Low-level lighting might be ideal for a home office, but it would be hopeless in a kitchen that requires lighting sufficiently bright for cooking. These are the reasons why we are about to look at decorating from the perspective of a room and its purpose. In each case we will look at how the different functions of each room will have a bearing on the colours, lighting and furniture that are chosen.

Halls, Corridors & Landings

How to make the most of the area that these spaces provide and to ensure they look their best.

Although these 'in-between' spaces of the home tend to be far down our list of decorating priorities, they have an important role, offering the first impression of an interior or the introduction to a room. Designers take three different approaches: the first option is to treat them as simple, artfully lit spaces; the second is to decorate them with discreet decorative elements such as mirrors and wall lights; the third is to treat them as a picture gallery.

KEY POINTS

✱ While console tables with lamps are visually appealing, you may decide that wall-mounted lighting offers a better use of space.

✱ Paint walls in colours that will help 'link' different rooms.

✱ Consider creating built-in storage in the 'dead space' in halls or landings.

OPPOSITE A classic hall and staircase have been given a contemporary edge with bold colour, a striped stair runner and a painted wooden floor.

BELOW With a combination of striped wallpaper, checked upholstery and traditional paint colours, this scheme has a period feel.

LAYOUT While many people regard halls and corridors as 'dead space', they can offer extra storage (particularly bookshelves), room for occasional dining or a home office. Remember, however, that their primary function is to offer easy movement through the house.

WALLS Be led by the style of the rooms leading off the space. If there are a number of different styles you may like to keep the look understated and the colours muted to create a cohesive feel. In the absence of natural light, don't rule out dark colours – the combination of dark tones and good artificial lighting can be very striking.

WINDOWS When not in use blinds maximize the amount of natural light that can enter a room and are less intrusive than curtains – however, heavy curtains do offer excellent insulation. If you want a light, airy feel look for places where roof lights could go.

LIGHTING Wall- or ceiling-mounted lights have many advantages over table lamps. For a simple, architectural look, consider installing recessed low-voltage spots. Wall-mounted lights create a more decorative look.

FLOORING A combination of hard flooring such as wood or stone with rugs and runners is the most practical option for high-traffic areas (wooden floors without rugs are extremely noisy). If you are opting for natural flooring, fit underlay to ensure durability.

ABOVE This landing has been given a light, airy feel by keeping the furnishings to a minimum. On landings and in halls and corridors you may decide that curtains and blinds are unnecessary.

ABOVE LEFT In the absence of a window, hanging the wall with a collection of mirrors – such as these decorative Venetian-style designs – will help to compensate for the lack of natural light

THIS PAGE A palette of greys, neutrals and a touch of gilt have been used to create a room that is classic in style but also has a fresh, contemporary feel. **OPPOSITE** A disparate combination of patterns add a quirky character to this otherwise neutral scheme.

Living Rooms

Whether you want a formal or a multifunctional living space, good planning is essential.

The style of a living room will be governed by the function you intend to fulfil it. This could be anything from a formal entertaining space to a home office or a children's room. If you intend the room only to be used occasionally you will have a greater opportunity to create a bold statement. A multi-purpose room will require a more complex arrangement and a cleaner more contemporary look to accommodate the various different activities.

KEY POINTS

* Wherever possible try to create a scheme that is symmetrical and that has a central focus such as a fireplace.
* In an open-plan, multifunctional room, use furniture or rugs to create areas for different activities such as dining or working.
* For a pared-down look limit the items stored in the room to those that are directly related to its purpose.
* A combination of different light sources is crucial.

LAYOUT Along with a kitchen, planning the layout of a living room will require the greatest thought. A scale drawing of the room plan with scale cut-outs of individual items of furniture will ensure that you get the most from the space. The rooms that will require the greatest thought are those with an open-plan space that is used for a variety of different activities such as watching television, working and eating. Using the arrangement of furniture to create

different areas for these activities is known as 'zoning'; other elements, such as rugs, can also be used to define zones. Typically, the seating area is arranged around a central focus such as a fireplace. Most designers believe that the more symmetrical the arrangement, the better the visual appearance. However, in the majority of cases any arrangement will be dictated by the architecture of the room. If space is limited try to eliminate too many secondary items such as occasional tables and magazine racks. Even if your arrangement isn't strictly symmetrical you can create a feeling of symmetry with, for example, a pair of accessories such as candlesticks on either side of a mantelpiece. If possible, restrict storage to items that are essential to the prime purpose of the room (such as television and hi-fi equipment) and banish items such as books to other rooms. The fewer non-essential items you have in the sitting room, the greater opportunity you'll have to create a room that is both functional and a bold style statement.

WINDOWS As a living room tends to be the place where you want to create a relaxed mood, well-insulated curtains or blinds are ideal. However, if the room is in a quiet location, without intrusive light, you might decide that the cost of heavy curtains might be invested in some other element. Alternatively you might decide to use window treatments such as plantation shuttersto make a bolder statement that enhances the overall scheme.

WALLS For many people, the walls of the living room also fulfil the role of art gallery. If so, then remember that unless you have artworks that are very simple in style, they will have a dominant impact on the room. One solution is to ensure that artworks have identical frames and that the arrangements are regimented. Also, decorate the walls on which pictures are hung

in a muted colour and avoid any pattern, unless it is very subtle. Alternatively, you may like the idea of banishing all but a few choice artworks to other parts of the house, such as the hallway and stairs. If you are keen to use a patterned wallpaper, remember that the living room is a place where you will spend a great deal of your time and you may quickly tire of anything that is too distinctive. For a discreetly luxurious look a paint finish or textured wallpaper is a good contemporary option.

LEFT When adding modern furniture to a classic scheme, use colour to harmonize the look.

BELOW Traditional fabrics add a distinctive French flavour to this country-style living room.

OPPOSITE Plenty of built-in storage is essential for a minimal look.

LIGHTING In a multifunctional room such as a living room try to achieve a wide range of lighting options. Aim for a combination of low level 'mood lighting' and overhead lighting for cleaning (ideally both should be on dimmers). The classic option is one overhead pendant light and table lamps. However, the latter can be limiting, primarily because a table lamp will necessitate a table that you might not otherwise have wished to incorporate into the scheme. In addition to this, the pendant lamp with a bare light bulb can seem intrusive – particularly if you want to achieve a sleek, contemporary look. Instead, you might wish to consider a combination of low floor lamps (that serve the same purpose as table lamps) and recessed low-voltage spotlights. Another type of lighting that will create a 'layered' look is wall-mounted lighting.

FLOORING Your choice really depends on how 'hard-working' you intend the room to be. For a formal room that is only used occasionally you have the flexibility to choose whatever suits the overall scheme, but for a room that is used by a number of people on a daily basis, a heavy-duty flooring is undoubtedly the most practical option.

STORAGE It is always best to limit storage to the essentials. Some people like to hide their television and hi-fi equipment behind cupboards, but in a modern living room a well-designed media system can be an attractive asset – although it is essential that wiring is discreet and that there are plenty of power sockets nearby. If you really want a minimal style remember that, with some planning, it is easy to keep the bulkier components such as a CD player and amplifier elsewhere. Alternatively, a fitted unit that incorporates a cupboard below and built-in bookcases above will offer enough storage for a hi-fi system. Televisions are harder to disguise – the only options are a TV cabinet or, to take off the hard edges of technology, an older piece such as an antique linen press.

Case Study Living Room

When planning a living room the secret to mixing furniture and accessories in a variety of different styles is to create harmony with a common colour theme. In this stylish scheme maximum impact is achieved by setting them against a plain, off-white backdrop.

WALLS The advantage of creating a cool backdrop is that it gives prominence to other integrated elements such as this large abstract acrylic.

ACCESSORIES Wherever possible give the room a cohesive feel by including items of glassware and ceramics that complement the overall scheme. The cushions on the sofa serve a similar purpose.

FURNITURE The soft colour and naturalistic, twig-like form of this side table form a decorative, but unobtrusive, part of the scheme.

COLOUR The combination of shades of cool blues, neutrals and whites have a harmonizing effect on the overall scheme.

TEXTURE The chair fabric combines the luxurious feel of flock velvet with the roughness of linen – an unlikely but successful pairing.

PATTERN Combining a graphic, contemporary fabric with a more classic pattern requires a good balance of colours.

FURNITURE Upholstering a classic sofa in a plain fabric will give it a contemporary look. The coffee table creates a discreetly modern touch.

FABRICS The look is softened with cushions and a throw in similar colours. Co-ordinating fabrics make a bold statement against a neutral backdrop.

FLOORING Fitted carpets in two different textures create a comforting feel.

Kitchens

Your kitchen needs to accommodate a variety of functions, from food preparation to entertaining.

More than any other room the design of your kitchen will be governed by its size. This is the reason that the objective of most contemporary designers is to maximize the amount of space available in order to create a kitchen that will accommodate as many activities as possible, including food preparation, entertaining and in some cases a variety of other activities from working to relaxing. There are, however, a number of ways to create a large kitchen: ideas range from sacrificing an adjoining room to adding a new one, often in the form of a conservatory. These are both expensive solutions and if you are not able to make the investment then you'll need to think laterally to make the most of the available space. One option is to minimize the amount of storage and number of appliances in the kitchen by devoting a smaller room to utilities such as a fridge, freezer and washing machine; this can also house plenty of shelves for kitchen equipment that is only used on an occasional basis.

It is important to recognize that in the absence of a huge budget, kitchen design is about compromise; when making decisions you will be expected to weigh up cost against aesthetics and practicality.

KEY POINTS

* Establish a comfortable route between areas for food preparation, serving and storage.
* Ideally a sink should face a window.
* If you have a large kitchen, try to avoid wall-mounted cupboards as these will reduce the feeling of open space.

RIGHT A combination of cool, neutral colours, plenty of natural light and a good use of space have created a room that is as suited to cooking as it is to entertaining.

OPPOSITE (CLOCKWISE FROM TOP LEFT) A combination of vibrant red and black give a bold look to this contemporary kitchen; a large island unit creates a convenient work space and plenty of storage in a generous-sized kitchen; a table and chairs are an essential addition to even the smallest kitchen; neutral colours give a calming feel to Shaker-style units.

LAYOUT The successful design of any kitchen – however big or small – relies on creating a triangle between three 'activity zones' for food preparation, cooking and serving, each with their own dedicated work surfaces, storage and appliances. For maximum efficiency the total length of the three sides of the triangle should be 3,600–6,600mm (12–21½ft) and wherever possible any movement should be uninterrupted by through traffic.

There are four basic layouts to consider:

Corridor: This layout is for long, narrow spaces. If you are planning to position rows of worktops and appliances opposite one another, you will need at least 1,200mm (4ft) between each row. If this isn't possible you should consider having worktops and appliances against just one wall.

L-shaped: This is the best solution for kitchens where it is possible for worktops and appliances to be installed in one corner.

U-shaped: This is the ideal layout as all appliances are then within easy reach. Ensure that there is at least 1,200 mm (4ft) between both sides of the U-shape.

Island: In a kitchen where there is plenty of room an island provides a central work space around which to manoeuvre. It is a popular format as it makes cooking a more sociable activity. If you choose to install appliances or a sink, remember that you will have to allow for the provision of plumbing and electricity.

Peninsula: When space is limited this layout offers many of the advantages of the island but the central work space is connected to the other units.

WINDOWS When planning a layout, remember that the kitchen sink is best positioned next to a window, as a view will provide a welcome distraction from washing-up. Window treatments should never detract from the kitchen's role as a functional machine. Blinds take up a minimum of space and you can choose a fabric that is easy to clean without washing.

WALLS When deciding on wall treatments, practicality is all. Above preparation areas there is no substitute for tiles – or the increasingly popular modern options of stainless steel or glass. For the rest of the kitchen you can choose almost anything, but remember that any walls near kitchen chairs will become scuffed, so you may wish to consider putting up a dado rail at the height at which the back of the chair will come in contact with the wall.

LIGHTING Because a kitchen accommodates a variety of functions a good range of lighting should be available. Preparation areas will require good 'task lighting' that is either positioned directly over work surfaces or which can be angled in their direction – low-voltage halogen bulbs create the most attractive light. A less expensive option is to fit strip lighting under eye-level units that create a pool of light over work surfaces. Depending on the layout and design of your kitchen these should also provide sufficient light for cleaning.

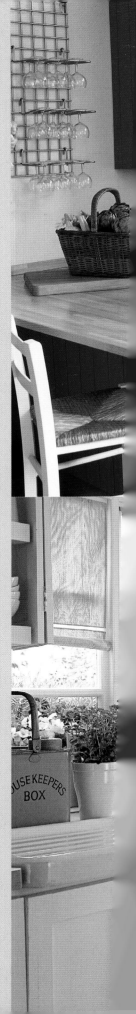

LEFT Open storage in a pale colour creates space and makes crockery easier to find.
BELOW LEFT This compact, contemporary kitchen is installed in the living room of a small flat.
OPPOSITE Increasingly, hardwoods are being used to inject colour and texture into kitchens.

If you intend to eat in your kitchen you will also need 'mood lighting' around the table that will create a more relaxed feel. It is also useful to be able to switch off lights in the kitchen preparation area when the kitchen is being used as a dining room.

FLOORING Floors, in the same way as walls, require a completely practical approach. While it is important to have a floor with an appealing appearance that fits with the style of your kitchen, it is more critical that whatever surface you choose is both water-resistant and easy to clean. These decisions will depend on how heavily the kitchen will be used. A kitchen that is exclusively used for food preparation by one person, for example, won't require the same heavyweight, easily maintained flooring as one that is also used as a dining room and is home to toddlers and family pets. If you have animals then linoleum, rubber or one of the synthetic alternatives will offer a better choice than stone or wood.

STORAGE Because kitchens are full of both equipment and accessories, methods of effective storage require considerable thought. The conventional approach is to fit a combination of base- and wall-mounted units, but an increasingly popular option is to create one large walk-in cupboard. There are two advantages to this arrangement. The first is that equipment and ingredients are more easy to find than in a series of individual cupboards. The second is that you can maintain a more open feel to the space by avoiding the use of wall-mounted units.

Case Study Kitchen

This kitchen not only provides plenty of efficient work space, but also storage and a place for casual meals. So the fact that it looks so calm and ordered makes its design an impressive feat. Invest plenty of time in planning and there's no reason why you shouldn't achieve the same solution.

WORK SURFACES A central island is a good use of open space and provides a sociable surface on which to prepare food.

FURNITURE A high kitchen table not only provides a place for informal meals but also additional storage in the form of drawers and space underneath.

STORAGE Although the kitchen is not particularly large, the creative approach to storage and layout has contributed to the clean, welcoming feel of this space. Limiting the number of eye-level units means that the room will appear spacious and won't feel too claustrophobic.

FURNITURE A bench with built-in storage is a way of providing space without fitting eye-level units, which often dominate the space.

SINKS If your budget allows, fit a second kitchen sink – one for washing dishes, and the other for preparing vegetables.

STORAGE Open shelves not only look decorative and eye-catching, they also offer a home for items that need to be easily accessible.

THIS PAGE The formal style and cool colour palette of a classic Swedish-style interior is a good source of inspiration for a dining-room scheme. **OPPOSITE** In open schemes a dining area can be successfully incorporated either into a kitchen or – as here – into a living room.

Dining Rooms

A combination of glamour and versatility is the best way of getting the most from a dining room.

For many people a dining room has become something of an anachronism; with the increasing popularity of the kitchen-dining room, using an entire room for the sole purpose of eating might seem like a waste of space. If you do decide to have a dedicated dining room remember that it can easily serve an additional purpose, such as a home office, in which case you should make a point of creating plenty of storage in which to hide papers and filing when you are entertaining.

KEY POINTS

∗ A dining table that can be extended offers flexibility – particularly if the room is small or is to be used for some other purpose.

∗ While soft lighting is ideal for entertaining, good overhead lighting is important for cleaning.

∗ Hang pictures at the eye level of a person who is sitting at the table rather than one at standing level.

∗ Make the most of any spare space with freestanding storage such as a dresser (hutch) or cupboard.

RIGHT In this period interior, simple furniture and minimal decoration create a refreshing contemporary feel.

OPPOSITE A period look is ideal for formal dining. A combination of large mirrors and crystal chandeliers are a classic way of maximizing light.

LAYOUT Planning the layout of a dining room around a large table will compromise the rest of the room. However large the room, a table of modest proportions that can be extended when necessary will give you greater flexibility, particularly if the room will be used for other purposes. If the room is just for occasional entertaining you could have a simple folding table that can be stored when not in use.

WINDOWS Your choice of window treatment will probably be governed by the style of the dining room rather than by any functional demands. For a clean, contemporary look simple blinds will do the trick. For a more glamorous style elaborate curtains are still popular. The traditional approach, particularly for period houses, is a complex treatment based on an ornamental curtain pole or a simpler design, with discreetly decorative detailing such as box pleating and fabrics such as bold damasks, stripes or pictorial fabrics. For a more contemporary feel use a combination of an elaborate curtain treatment with a plain fabric, preferably one with plenty of texture such as velvet or a heavy linen. The look can work extremely well, even in an otherwise contemporary scheme.

WALLS While formal stripes or deep, traditional reds are popular, this is another element that can be simple as well as glamorous. A paint finish or wallpaper with a slightly metallic sheen or texture will create depth and interest instead of matt flatness. Pictures also help to enhance any overall theme – but they should always be hung at the eye level of a seated person.

LIGHTING While an elaborate centrally placed chandelier hung over a dining table is a popular option, if you have a low ceiling it can be very distracting, particularly if you decide to use the room for some other purpose such as a home office. For a similarly decorative look you could also consider elaborate wall lights. Never overlook the need for overhead lights for use when cleaning or during any other activity requiring good general illumination.

FLOORING Practicality, particularly where children are concerned, is a prime consideration; allowing you to be more relaxed about any food and wine spills. Even if you have carpets or natural flooring in the rest of the house, there is a convincing argument for a hardwood or painted floor in the dining area. Also, because much of the flooring will be covered by a table, it will have less impact on the rest of the scheme than in any other room. If you choose a fitted floorcovering, consider a dark coloured rug under the table.

STORAGE A dining room will not require a large storage space, although any surplus space can be useful for storing items that are unrelated to dining. A traditional dresser (hutch) is one solution – they don't occupy much space and look decorative. To maximize storage you could use full-height built-in cupboards. However, if these are too intrusive a pair of built-in or freestanding waist-high cupboards will be useful. With a glass top they can also be used for serving food.

Case Study Dining Room

Increasingly, devoting a room exclusively to eating and entertaining is seen as a luxury. However, creating a multifunctional space with plenty of storage means that you can get the best out of this useful room. Here, a combination of simple floral patterns and complementary accent colours create an artful blend of traditional and contemporary.

WALLS An inspiring example of one of the new ways in which wallpaper is now being used in contemporary interiors. Two lengths of wallpaper have been mounted side by side in frames, creating a decorative effect that is far more subtle than when wallpaper is hung on all four walls. An alternative option for a modern interior is to hang wallpaper on one wall only and then to paint the others in a complementary colour.

WINDOWS These simple curtains have been given a luxurious touch with the addition of two parallel rows of braid – you could also use fabric borders or fringing. A simple blind in the window with a beaded fringe allows you to control light and create privacy without drawing the curtains.

TABLE When choosing a tablecloth it sometimes pays to think laterally – here, a white quilted fabric gives a wonderful textured feel.

ACCESSORIES A combination of white tableware with glassware in an accent colour creates a stylish effect. In this room the colour is picked up in the curtains, walls and tableware as well as the potted and cut flowers.

WALLS The wallpaper is mounted in frames that can either be fixed to the wall or lent against them for a more casual look.

Home Office

Create the ideal space in which to work from home
– or one where you can simply organize your finances.

The old-fashioned name for this room is a study, but with growing numbers
working from home its use has changed considerably. What distinguishes
the home office from its older format is that it has to incorporate far more
technology. Even when telephones, wiring and filing are resolved, the bigger
challenge of achieving a well-designed scheme still remains. In most cases
a built-in desk and shelving offers the most effective use of space. The
latter is also important if you want to create a compact work space so that
the rest of the room can be used for another purpose, such as a spare
bedroom or dining room. If space is at a premium compact home offices
can also be incorporated into living rooms, halls, landings or corridors.

KEY POINTS

* Built-in storage – however rudimentary – will make the best use of
  space and offer a more efficient way to organize books and files
* If you don't have the space to devote an entire room to a home office,
  incorporate it into another room such as a bedroom.
* The look doesn't have to be functional – with clever planning, period
  furniture can be converted to provide efficient storage and work space.

OPPOSITE Oriental-style furniture gives an exotic look to this home office.
THIS PAGE When planning a home office consider updating a period piece of furniture by painting it in a cool, neutral colour.

OPPOSITE Work space has been
created here in the area beneath
a flight of stairs.
BELOW Here colour has been injected
into an otherwise functional scheme
with a boldly patterned fabric.

LAYOUT A popular layout is a long built-in desk that runs the entire length of one wall, providing plenty of work space, with filing cabinets beneath on castors.

WALLS On walls above desks, create a combination of noticeboards and shelving; this will create extra space for easily accessible files and books.

WINDOWS If possible, the desk should face a window – it is much better to work in natural rather than artificial light.

LIGHTING Because in a home office you will principally need task lighting, such as an Anglepoise, positioned over the desk, you might decide that expensive overhead lighting is an unnecessary investment. For cleaning, you will need one overhead light.

FLOORS If you have an office chair and filing cabinets on castors, it might be more practical to have a hard floorcovering, such as vinyl or linoleum rather than carpets or rugs.

STORAGE For ease of access, open storage is far more convenient than cupboards. However, for a more streamline look it is worth planning a fitted, integrated system rather than several individual units.

Case Study
Home Office

With more people working from home a dedicated office is a useful asset. The style doesn't have to be quite as functional as a corporate office, so you can soften the look with pattern and accessories. If you don't have the space for a dedicated office, why not combine it with a dining room or bedroom?

DESK A built-in desk provides an inexpensive, functional place to work and allows plenty of room for storage underneath. The least expensive options are melamine or MDF, but a hardwood surface would inject texture and colour.

STORAGE A combination of open shelving and drawers provides all the necessary storage for a study. Open shelving provides the most convenient access to books and files.

WINDOWS While a home office will inevitably have quite a functional appearance, it is possible to soften the look by introducing a bold splash of pattern and colour.

WALLS Much of the wall space will be devoted to shelving, however a noticeboard is a useful addition to a home office. This one has been covered in a striped fabric that complements the colours of the blinds.

FURNITURE While a chair mounted on castors is the most functional option, consider adding more decorative pieces, such as a comfortable chair for reading and a standard lamp that will create a soft pool of light in the evening?

FLOORS Chairs with castors operate far more effectively on hard floors than they do on carpets. Choose between a surface of wood, vinyl or linoleum.

Bedrooms

How to create a comfortable oasis of calm
and tranquility at bed time.

There are two schools of thought among decorators. The first is that
because a bedroom isn't a 'public' area such as a living or dining room,
you should have the freedom to choose a decorating style that is more
adventurous than the rest of the house. This is the reason that the
bedrooms of many homes have walls decorated with vibrant patterns,
particularly florals, because their owners might have lacked the courage
to use such bold designs elsewhere in the house.

The second view is that a bedroom should be a calm retreat from the
rest of the house; in this scenario there should be nothing to distract you
from relaxation and sleep. To this end, colours are kept calm (often cream
or off-white), pattern is at a minimum and furniture is as simple as possible.
There is a half-way house between these two extremes; a good option is
a mixture of a striking item of furniture, such as an elaborate four-poster
bed, hung with plain fabrics and offset with richly coloured walls.

Whichever style you choose, there are a number of essential
ingredients for every bedroom: comfort, darkness, silence and storage.
These key factors should be tackled right from the outset. For example,
if you are intent on creating a quiet bedroom then consider its position
in the house and decide whether another room might offer a more tranquil
space. Alternatively, if you love the comfort and convenience of an en-suite
bathroom, you might decide that it is worth sacrificing a small adjoining
room to make this possible. It is essential that you approach the room
within the context of the house rather than on its own.

KEY POINTS

* Always use the position of the bed as the starting point of any scheme,
  it will have a bearing on almost every other element in the room.
* In noisy areas or areas with plenty of light it is essential to hang heavy
  curtains with blackout lining.
* If you have limited space, consider creating clothes storage elsewhere.
* If you have a great deal of space consider creating a walk-in cupboard.

RIGHT A combination of a neutral
scheme and exotic hardwoods give
this room a dramatic colonial look.

BEDROOMS IN ROOF EXTENSIONS

Building a roof extension is an increasingly popular way to add habitable space to a house, especially to terrace houses. This involves raising the height of the walls of a house and adding windows (these take the form of either roof lights or dormer windows, or a combination of the two).

A bedroom in a roof extension can present a unique set of design challenges. One of the chief problems is that because of the pitch of the roof there are plenty of jarring angles to cope with. The obvious approach is to create a simple scheme in one colour. The traditional – and somewhat braver – solution is to create a distraction from the awkwardness of the space by hanging a bold, patterned wallpaper. In this case it makes sense to keep the paintwork, the flooring and the bed linen as muted at possible – or to choose a colour that co-ordinates with the dominant colour in the wallpaper.

The other problem is awkwardly shaped windows, for which conventional window treatments are impractical. Standard roof lights are the most straightforward because it is possible to buy blinds made by the manufacturer (but these are likely to differ from the fabrics that you choose to use elsewhere in the scheme). In order to cope with the logistics of the pitched roof, larger windows often have irregular designs, making curtains impossible. In most cases the best solution is a system of bespoke blinds. Remember, however, that if you choose roller blinds there is a limit to the combined weight of the fabric and any lining you choose.

PLANNING A LAYOUT WHEN SPACE IS LIMITED

Start by tackling three key issues: the size of your bed, its position in the room and the locations of any existing or planned storage. Whenever possible, it is good to try to minimize the amount of furniture in a bedroom, even if space isn't a problem. This isn't purely a question of logistics – if you want to create a calm, uncluttered atmosphere then less is definitely more. The single element that compromises the design of many bedrooms is storage; yet even in the smallest home, it might be possible to create flexible storage space elsewhere.

ABOVE Fabrics in greys and charcoals create a distinctly, masculine feel in this bedroom. A wall-mounted mirror encourages the feeling of space. On the walls, black-and-white photographs enhance the look.

BELOW Grey paintwork, furniture and bed linen create a cool, sophisticated style in this classic bedroom. Bare walls always produce a calmer feel than those hung with a complex arrangement of pictures.

ABOVE A combination of classic painted furniture and French-style fabrics give this room a relaxed, elegant look. The bench at the foot of the bed provides a place to sit while changing or to place luggage when packing.

BELOW A four-poster bed makes a dramatic statement. Soft colours such as creams, whites and pale blues will ensure that the effect isn't too overbearing. Here, a leopard-print fabric adds an exotic quality.

A good place to look for additional storage space is in a spare bedroom, or in the 'dead' space on a landing which can be exploited with the help of cleverly designed built-in cupboards. Alternatively, by 'editing' down the clothes you need on a daily basis and storing items only used occasionally in an attic or garage, you will need less extensive storage.

The secret to a successful layout in a small bedroom is to turn a compromise into a virtue. For example, banishing storage and limiting furniture just to a bed – even if it means placing a double bed so that one side is facing a wall – might mean that you will be able to accommodate a larger, more comfortable bed. When planning, simply trade off one advantage or disadvantage against another.

During the decision-making process, a worthwhile exercise is to put your bed in the intended position and sleep in it for a few nights to see how it works.

PLANNING A LAYOUT WHEN YOU HAVE SPACE TO SPARE Even if you have a large amount of space at your disposal, you may not wish to fill it with furniture. However, if you want to use your room as a retreat – perhaps for reading, working or watching television – you might introduce an armchair, chaise longue or a small desk to reinforce your intended use of the space (if space is limited elsewhere in the house you may also consider creating a home office with discreet storage for files). In some cases – particularly in a roof extension – you might decide that you have so much room that you can use some of it for a new bathroom or walk-in dressing room.

WINDOWS When considering how to dress bedroom windows, remember that the main function of curtains and blinds is to insulate a room from light, noise and cold or, in the summer, from heat (in addition to providing privacy). It is for this reason that bedroom curtains and blinds should not simply be regarded as a decorative accessory; in order to ensure a good night's (or afternoon's sleep) they must function perfectly. A number of factors should dictate your choice. For example, a bedroom with double-glazed windows in a quiet location where there is no light from street lamps shouldn't require heavyweight

RIGHT Tongue-and-groove panelling, a traditional iron bed and a patchwork quilt give this country-style guest bedroom a nostalgic charm.
OPPOSITE Open storage for items of clothing that are used daily will make dressing quicker and easier.

curtains or blinds, while one with old-fashioned sash windows at the front of a house on a busy highway almost certainly will.

The curtains that offer the most effective insulation from the elements are those made from a heavyweight fabric, with both an outer and a thick inner lining (known as interlining) plus a blackout lining which eradicates all light.

The traditional solution to the problem of privacy is a pair of net curtains. There are, however, plenty of other alternatives ranging from etched glass (or the less expensive option of windows that have been treated with an adhesive film or spray to look as if they have been etched) to slatted 'plantation' shutters.

For a clean, contemporary look, you may decide that simple blinds are the best option. Be aware, however, that they won't offer the same level of insulation as curtains – much will depend on the position of the room and the type of windows.

In an extreme situation where there is an excess of noise and light (for example where there is a combination of heavy traffic and a street lamp outside the window) you might want to consider shutters. Reclaimed shutters – or those that are period in style – can be an expensive option. Simple MDF shutters are cheaper, if less visually appealing. You might also look at combining them with curtains, particularly if you choose functional-looking shutters that aren't in keeping with the rest of the room.

An increasingly popular option is a pair of folding plantation shutters – these have the advantage of allowing you to control the amount of natural light in a room and offer privacy during the day.

WALLS Cool, calm colours are now the most popular option for bedroom walls, but you could choose something bolder, maybe a pictorial wallpaper such as toile de Jouy. A classic but expensive option is to line the walls in fabric; this creates a cosseted, cocoon-like atmosphere because the fabric absorbs sound. Fabrics will certainly offer a far greater variety of designs.

LIGHTING Planning a lighting scheme for a bedroom is a relatively straightforward business, but the same central rule applies to this room as much as any other – research and planning. Only when you are sure of the position of the bed should you fit or rearrange sockets. Putting the bed in its proposed position, will help you to visualize the amount of lighting required.

While the conventional choice for bedside lighting is a small lamp on a bedside table, you might also consider the contemporary option of a wall-mounted

or freestanding light and forgo a bedside table altogether. As well as creating a sleeker look it is also ideal when space is limited or if you have a low bed such as a futon. The ideal – and inexpensive – option is a simple Anglepoise lamp.

Another contemporary solution is to create a recessed 'niche' the same width as the bed, at the top of which is a hidden strip light that will provide a soft, diffused light at the head of the bed. Whichever of these options you choose, ensure that any new wiring systems will allow you to turn lights on and off from a switch by the door.

Bedside lighting isn't the only type that you will need in a bedroom. Some type of overhead lighting is also essential cleaning and packing, especially if there is limited natural light.

The more discreet alternative to a pendant light or chandelier are low-voltage spotlights that create a more evenly spread light source. You may also want to create a combination of light sources for a 'layered' effect with eye-level wall lights. Whichever you choose, remember to install a dimmer switch to create the maximum number of options.

FLOORING Deep-pile fitted carpets offer the most comfort underfoot. However, if you are attracted to the clean look of hard flooring you can always soften these floors with wool or cotton rugs. Alternatively, a good compromise is natural flooring.

STORAGE There is considerable advantage in banishing storage from the bedroom, but if this isn't possible ensure that it is as sleek and unobtrusive as possible. Simple built-in floor-to-ceiling cupboards without any detailing tend to be the best option. If you have the space, a large, antique, freestanding cupboard will be the most cost-effective option (some designers believe that filling a small room with one or two items of large furniture will make it look bigger than a greater number of small items). When planning storage take advantage of the fact that underbed storage offers an excellent, discreet solution, particularly for bulky items such as blankets and woollens.

Case Study Bedroom

Banishing storage and creating a neutral colour scheme are two ways of creating a calm, restful bedroom. In addition, incorporating one or two comfortable pieces of furniture, such as a large armchair, will help to make a space that is a comfortable haven, away from the trappings of everyday life.

BED A four-poster bed doesn't have to be elaborate – this simple bed creates a formal look without including swathes of fabric. In winter you could create a snugger look by hanging curtains around the bed.

FLOOR Soften the look of wooden floors, with deep-pile, textural rugs.

WALLS White walls, alongside an almost exclusively white scheme, can create a calm, serene atmosphere in a bedroom.

FURNITURE A bench at the foot of the bed offers a useful place to sit when getting dressed or to place luggage while packing and unpacking.

FURNITURE An armchair and matching footstool are always useful additions to a bedroom – either for reading or as a place to leave clothes overnight. This antique chair has been given a fresh, contemporary feel with a simple white fabric.

FIREPLACE A fireplace that is the same colour as the walls provides a restrained architectural detail in this otherwise simple interior.

FURNITURE In this room almost the only colour other than white is gold. This is a good example of how an opulent material such as gold can take on quite a different character when it is seen in a cool, white contemporary setting than a classic interior.

LIGHTING This elaborate glass chandelier adds a discreet decorative element in an otherwise plain scheme.

Bathrooms

Combining comfort and practicality will create
a bathroom that looks and feels good.

There is a new dynamic in bathroom design. In just the same way as the
kitchen was regarded as a purely functional part of the house fifty years
ago, the emphasis is now on creating a more luxurious environment.
Devoting extra room to a bathroom is useful, but by no means essential,
for creating a luxurious feel. It is more critical to ensure that you maximize
the space you already have. An interesting new development has been the
evolution of the shower into a 'wet room'; this effectively makes the idea
of the enclosed shower redundant by using a combination of drainage and
a waterproof membrane in the walls. There are certain regulations that
apply to bathrooms, such as the fact that external ventilation is required,
either with a window or an extractor fan, and a bathroom with a toilet
must not open directly off a kitchen.

KEY POINTS

✳ Stick to prescribed rules about the amount of space that you need to
  allow beside and alongside showers, bathtubs and sinks (see page 155).
✳ Wherever possible, try to create open shelving in 'dead space' such
  as alcoves.
✳ For an open-plan look consider creating a wet room.

RIGHT Fitting a bathtub into the
chimney breast and the sink into
the alcove has made the most of the
available space. A floral fabric adds
colour and pattern to an otherwise
muted interior.

LAYOUT Because a bathroom design is governed by the need to balance three or four essential elements – bathtub, toilet, sink and possibly a shower – the planning process should start with a detailed scale drawing. And, since the business of moving water and power supply and drainage can have significant cost implications, establish these plans from the outset.

The suggested working space to allow for a bathtub is 1100 x 700mm (43 x 27in) alongside with 2200mm (86½in) of headroom; there should be 200mm (8in) on either side of a sink and 700mm (27in) in front; and 900 x 700mm (35½ x 27in) on each side of a shower.

Also plan other features such as an electric shaver point, mirror (possibly with a light), extractor fan and bathroom cabinet, as well as other optional items such as a laundry basket, chair or stool, and shelving.

PLANNING THE LAYOUT OF A LARGE BATHROOM If you have plenty of space in your bathroom a pair of sinks are the ultimate in luxury. You may also choose to include items of furniture such as an upholstered chair or sofa – these will be certain to add a luxurious feel.

WINDOWS Your choice will be governed by the space available. Blinds are ideal in a small bathroom as they take up a minimum of space and allow window ledges to be used as storage.

WALLS Aesthetically and practically tiles are one of the best wallcovering, but they are not the only solution, particularly in a room used by adults. In small bathrooms mirrors or mirror tiles will enhance the feeling of space.

LIGHTING Use a combination of recessed low-voltage halogen lights and wall lights near the mirror.

FLOORING The most practical flooring in a bathroom is vinyl or linoleum. There are new types of waterproof wooden floor that are also suitable for bathrooms.

STORAGE Good storage is key to a well-designed bathroom. Even when space is limited use any niches or alcoves to create storage for towels and cosmetics.

OPPOSITE Mosaic tiles give a luxurious look to a shower room. **BELOW** Traditional white tiles create a spotless, minimal style in this bathroom.

ABOVE 'Plantation' shutters create privacy without cluttering the space with curtains or blinds. A simple bowl-shaped sink sits on a wall-mounted counter.

Case Study Bathroom

One of the best ways to achieve a bathroom scheme that is functional and restful is to create an open-plan layout that is devoid of clutter. Richly coloured wood, stone and ceramic will ensure that the overall look isn't too austere.

LAYOUT Banishing clutter from a bathroom, or rather providing alternative storage areas, can make the most of the available space.

BATHTUB Thanks to a growing number of water-resistant treatments, wood is an increasingly popular option for bathroom interiors. The most obvious advantage is that it creates warmth, both to look at and to touch. Here, it has been used to create the tub surround, the vanity unit and the low bench. It adds a luxurious feel to what might otherwise become an unforgiving, austere interior.

SINKS A pair of sinks are the ultimate in luxury for couples. Here, two large square sinks have been installed on a sleek wall-mounted support.

WINDOW In the interests of creating a clean, pared-down look you may decide not to have blinds or curtains. If this is the case, glazing a window with etched glass is an effective device to ensure privacy.

FLOOR A stone, ceramic or composite floor will crreate a sleek, masculine look.

SHOWER By creating drainage and a waterproof floor, an 'open-plan' shower can be created so that a shower surround won't be required. This requires the fitting of a waterproof membrane beneath the floor.

WALLS Mosaic tiling is less expensive – and easier to fit – than you might expect. It can create a much more luxurious, exotic feel than conventional tiles. Here, slate grey creates a cool contemporary look.

Children's Bedrooms & Playrooms

Create a flexible space that will evolve to suit the different stages in a child's life.

When designing a room for a child, always plan with an eye on the future. The rapid speed at which children develop means that their rooms must have the capacity to evolve; within a couple of years a newborn baby's nursery will have to accommodate the needs of a toddler, and before very long a child whose taste may revolve around anything from dolls' houses to Lego. These requirement changes will stretch right into early adulthood.

The best approach may therefore be to create a blank canvas that will accommodate each new period in a child's life. This will mean that you should avoid decorating a baby's room in a stereotypical nursery style, however tempting the prospect. Instead, an anonymous, discreetly decorative look will allow you to offer a more enduring scheme. The same applies to furniture; for example, once a child has outgrown a cot it is possible to buy a bed that will last until adulthood. If this approach seems too inflexible, it needn't be. The secret is to respond to a child's changing tastes and interests with new bed linen and accessories.

KEY POINTS

* A neutral backdrop with colourful bed linen and accessories will be easier and less expensive to update.
* While fitted storage is ideal, transparent plastic boxes on shelves are a practical, inexpensive alternative.
* Flooring should be hard-wearing and easy to maintain.
* Add blackout lining to curtains and blinds in a baby's room.

RIGHT A simply executed paint design for the walls creates drama and also personalizes the two halves of this shared bedroom. The stripe theme unifies the whole scheme.

LAYOUT Flexibility is everything. In the same way as the best living rooms and kitchens are those that can accommodate a variety of activities, a child's room should serve as a place to sleep, play, work and read. Because plenty of floor space gives more flexibility, many people opt for a bunk bed over a desk and sitting area, maximizing the available space in the rest of the room. Another increasingly popular option is a built-in bed with storage below.

WINDOWS The rules for children's bedroom windows are similar to those in any other bedroom. When choosing curtains or blinds for a baby's room, include blackout lining, which is the only way to ensure that a room is completely dark in daylight.

WALLS If you are taking a long-term view with your decorating approach, it makes sense to choose a plain backdrop onto which you can hang pictures. For the sake of preserving wall surfaces, an effective idea is to fix a large area of cork on the wall to put up drawings or other artwork. Alternatively, you could paint an area of wall with a coat of blackboard paint to provide a permanent blackboard.

LIGHTING Use good overhead lighting such as low-voltage spots. For safety, always fit dummy plugs in the plug sockets.

FLOORING It would be a pity to hamper a child's creativity by laying an expensive, hard-to-maintain

OPPOSITE Simple open storage in the alcoves of this room provides versatile storage for clothes, books and toys.
RIGHT A fabric-covered futon by the window offers both seating and, when unfolded, a bed for an overnight guest.
BELOW RIGHT When choosing flooring, be practical – in this room painted wooden boards offer an inexpensive solution that can easily be refreshed with a new coat of paint.

floorcovering. A hard floor covered with rugs will offer the greatest combination of comfort, flexibility and practicality. However, if you decide to fit a carpet or natural flooring in a child's room, ensure that it is easily cleaned – it might, instead, be more practical to use floor tiles that can be replaced.

STORAGE If your budget will allow, built-in storage will make the best use of the available space. However, easy access is paramount; for toy storage use simple shelves fitted into an alcove, each holding a row of baskets or transparent storage boxes of a uniform size and style. For the sake of tidiness, you may decide to install a curtain pole towards the front of the alcove and hang a neutral-coloured curtain from it.

Case Study Child's Bedroom

The secret to creating a child's room is to create a multifunctional space that can easily be transformed at regular intervals so that it keeps up to date with constantly changing tastes and interests. This simple scheme provides plenty of storage with a neutral palette that offers opportunities for a girl to express her individuality.

FURNITURE Built-in furniture almost always makes the best of the available space. As well as a built-in bed, this girl's room also has a built-in sofa that is made comfortable for reading or relaxation with an upholstered pad and matching bolsters.

COLOUR Creating a neutral scheme means that the room's style can easily be adapted and updated as your growing child's tastes change.

STORAGE The clear advantage of using bespoke built-in furniture is that you can ensure that it provides plenty of useful storage.

STORAGE Open shelves mean that books and toys are easier to find. When planning cupboards, create a flexible system of drawers and hanging space – when children are young they tend only to have a few items of clothing that require a hanging rail.

COLOUR Introducing splashes of colour to a neutral scheme creates a new look without the expense of redecoration.

WALLS Hanging a fabric-covered noticeboard on a wall gives welcome elements of colour, and also saves wall finishes from being damaged by other more improvised methods of attaching pictures and cards.

FURNITURE Inexpensive small-scale furniture will encourage creativity, and will mean that children can paint and draw without supervision. Here, the painted chair adds another cheerful splash of colour.

8

The Knowledge

Even if you never become a dedicated do-it-yourself expert there are times when, for reasons of either budget or convenience, you decide to pick up a paint brush, a pair of scissors or an electric drill. With a combination of the right tools and a methodical approach, you'll find that many tasks are much easier than you imagined. Mastering even the most basic skills, such as creating a curtain heading or hanging wallpaper, will give you a new skill and a new experience of the decorating process. Better still, hands-on experience will make you aware of what is and isn't possible and the knowledge you gain will put you in a stronger position when you need to hire a professional.

And who knows? Trying your hand at one of these projects may give you the confidence to try something more complex.

Painting

Practical advice on getting the painting done, covering the entire process from clearing the space to applying the final coat.

Although you can be forgiven for imagining that painting a room is a combination of vigorous rolling and nifty brushwork, in fact those activities are just a tiny part of the whole process and the bulk of the work should be invested in preparation. However deft you are with a brush, if you're painting onto an uneven, unstable or ill-prepared surface all your hard work will come to nothing. Almost as important is the quality of your tools; true, as the adage goes, bad craftsmen blame their tools, but a good painter doesn't have a hope of doing a good job with a cheap brush that moults hairs with every stroke. Think of preparation and painting as two different activities and make sure that you never start one until you are completely satisfied with the other.

PREPARATION

BEFORE YOU BEGIN

There is preparation to do before you start any work on the surfaces to be painted. The clearer the space in which you have to work the better job you will do, so start by removing furniture and place any remaining items in the centre of the room covered in dust sheets. Remove curtains, lampshades, wall brackets and carpets (it is advisable to do this even if they are fitted).

SURFACE PREPARATION

You need to create a sound base on which to paint. The preparation required will depend on the type of surface and the state it is in. Most sound surfaces can simply be prepared with a combination of sugar soap and water. If you need to strip off the wallpaper, soften it first with a solution of wallpaper paste and detergent (add a handful of cellulose paste to each bucket of water – it helps to hold the water on the wall). For best results you may find it easier to use a steam stripper.

Fill any cracks or blemishes in the wood or plaster with an interior filler (in the case of new wood, add knotting so that the resin doesn't 'bleed'). Then finely roughen, or 'key', wooden surfaces before painting using fine-grade sandpaper. If you are painting bare wood or plaster, it is essential to prepare the surface with primer.

CALCULATING QUANTITIES

As a rule of thumb, all-purpose primer, undercoat, emulsion (latex) and gloss will cover between 12 and 16 metres per litre (300 sq ft per gallon). The texture of the surface will effect the amount of paint you use, so always over-estimate (it is useful to have extra for repairs).

TOOLS OF THE TRADE

As well as choosing the best-quality tools that you can afford, aim to choose a wide selection that will give the best chance of coping with every eventuality – this is particularly important in the case of brushes and scrapers.

* Cotton dust sheets to cover floors and furniture
* A good selection of scrapers and strippers
* A filling knife
* A wire brush
* Fine-grade sandpaper
* A combination ladder that doubles as a stepladder and stairwell ladder. This should have a locking hinge that is high enough to reach, but not higher than, the ceiling
* Depending on the nature of the job you might also want to buy or hire a blowtorch or hot-air stripper – the latter is a much safer option as there is no naked flame

PAINTING CEILINGS

To create the best finish, your head should be around 8cm (3in) from the ceiling when painting. If you don't like working at a height, you can choose to add a long handle to the roller to paint the main areas and then use steps to paint the corners and above the doors. If possible, remove light fittings and paint the ceiling in strips, in just the same way as you would mow a lawn. Always protect your head and hair from paint splashes.

PAINTING WALLS

If you are using a roller to paint walls in a horizontal direction, each band should be around 60cm (2ft) deep. If you are using a brush, then paint blocks that are about a fifth of a square meter (2 foot square). If you are right-handed start at the top right corner, and if you are left-handed start at the top left corner. Paint from the top and work down the wall before starting at the top again.

PAINT EFFECTS

In addition to using paint to create 'flat colours', another choice is to use combinations of oil-based colours that have been diluted with white spirit – known as glazes – to create a variety of different paint effects such as sponging, ragging, dragging and stippling. Before applying a paint effect you need to paint the surface with an oil-based undercoat or eggshell (never use gloss paint as the glaze won't stick to it). To create a glaze you need to buy a scumble glaze – a 2.5 litre tin will cover a room of around 3.5 sq m (1 gallon to cover a room of around 350 sq ft). The glaze is then coloured either with oil colours or a stainer. Start by adding a tiny amount of colour to the white spirit and then add the mixture to the glaze and test it on the surface. If you aren't happy, dilute or add more colour (or another colour) according to the type or depth of colour that you want. When making up a glaze, it is essential to have more than you need as it is almost impossible to create the same colour twice. For the best results the texture of the glaze should be liquid but quite viscous. If the glaze begins to thicken as you work, dilute it with a tiny amount of white spirit to return it to its former consistency.

Because paint finishes aren't as robust as paint that comes straight from the tin, it can be a good idea to coat the finish with a clear varnish to protect it an make it more durable.

Never add such a coating until the paint finish itself is completely dry. Also remember that glaze is flammable, so ensure that any cloths covered in it are kept in airtight containers until they are discarded.

Glazes can be used to create a variety of effects. The following are descriptions of the basic techniques, but it is inevitable that you will develop your own methods as you start to work. Before embarking on a new technique, experiment either on a wall that you plan to repaint or on a piece of wood that is painted in the same base colour. This preparation gives you the chance to master the technique and also allows you to understand just how the colour and consistency of the glaze will affect the final appearance of the paint finish.

RAGGING

This effect is created by brushing a strip of glaze that is the height of the wall and then removing some of it by manipulating the paint with a succession of crumpled-up rags so that it has a soft, textured appearance.

DRAGGING

This technique involves thinning the glaze down a great deal before applying it to the height of the wall and then quickly dragging a brush down the length of it.

SPONGING

This soft, dappled effect is achieved by dipping a sponge in a paint tray filled with glaze and then gently applying the sponge to the wall in a circular motion. Working in a circular movement means that the effect will be irregular. It is also possible to added a second colour to create a soft, tonal effect.

STIPPLING

This effect is similar in principle to sponging, but involves creating a uniform pattern by applying paint with a stippling brush.

STENCILLING

This technique involves using either your own or pre-cut plastic stencils to create patterns on the wall. Having taped the stencil in place with masking tape, use an oil-based paint crayon to rub paint onto an uncut area of the stencil. Next, work the paint into the brush using a circular motion and then brush the paint lightly into the cut-out areas.

PAINT GLOSSARY

EGGSHELL

Refers to an oil-based paint with a silky finish suitable for interior walls and woodwork.

EMULSION (LATEX)

Water-based paint for walls and ceilings.

FLAT OR DEAD-FLAT OIL

Provides a completely flat, oil-based finish. Generally used on walls but not used on areas of high wear.

GLOSS

Paint with a high sheen that is usually used on woodwork

SATIN OR SILK

Water-based vinyl or acrylic paint for walls in high-wear areas. A satin finish tends to be somewhat shinier than silk.

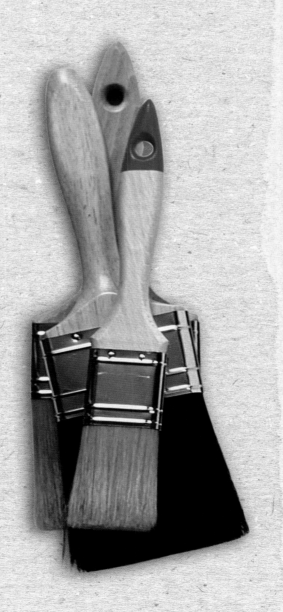

TOOLS FOR PAINTING

* For most painting jobs you will need a selection of paint brushes in the following sizes: 13mm (½in), 25mm (1in), 50mm (2in) and 150mm (6in); you will also need an angled 19mm (¾in) cutting in brush which is useful for painting window frames.
* A roller, preferably mohair, with extension
* A roller tray
* A radiator brush
* A paint kettle (never work from the tin)
* A paint stirrer
* Rags for cleaning up spills

TOOLS FOR CREATING PAINT EFFECTS

* Paint kettle (for making glazes)
* PVC gloves
* Mixing jar for thinning colours
* 10cm (4in) paint brush (for applying base paint)
* Sponge (for sponging)
* Flogger brush (for dragging)
* Stippling brush (for stippling)

Extracts taken from *Reader's Digest Complete DIY Manual*, courtesy of Reader's Digest Ltd.

Curtains & Blinds

You can get curtains and blinds tailor-made, but if you have a sewing machine and a reasonably simple design, then why not make them yourself?

MAKING CURTAINS

There are a huge number of curtain styles from which to choose, from basic unlined designs with simple ties to elaborate arrangements of fabrics. The design you select will depend largely on the purpose of the curtain (for example unlined curtains would not be suitable for a bedroom where heavyweight fabric and lining would be essential). The curtain suggested here is a relatively complicated design, but it is one that can always be simplified to suit your needs. Heading tape provides the mechanism that will pleat the curtain at the top – this comes in a variety of different options. The tape used here will create a triple pleat that creates a smart, all-purpose heading.

1 If there is no track or pole in place, choose a design and fit it first. Start by measuring the width of the window, taking into account how far the track or pole projects on either side. The wider the window, the longer the projection should be. Next, multiply the width by 2.25 for fullness, or 1.5 if you're planning to have tab-top eyelet headings, and add allowances for side hems and joining widths. Divide this measurement by the width of your fabric to calculate how many widths are required and then round up the final figure to the next full width. Measure the desired finished length of your curtains and add a minimum of 25cm (10in) for hem allowance and turnings at the top of the curtains (if the fabric is patterned, add the depth of the pattern repeat to the drop). Finally, multiply the number of widths by the length, plus allowances, to give you the total number of metres or yards of fabric required.

2 When cutting out each length either follow the pattern of the fabric or pull a thread out to use as a cutting guide. If you are using patterned fabric try to ensure that any incomplete motifs fall in the gathered heading. Mark across the fabric on the wrong side along the base of the motifs and measure from the hem allowance below this line and cut across the fabric. Then measure up from the cut edge to the correct length required for the curtains and cut across the fabric.

POLES, TRACKS & PELMETS

The way that you choose to hang your curtains is more than just a practical consideration, as it will also have an impact on how the room looks. The choice is between decorative metal or wooden poles and tracks whcih can be used with pelmets to create a neat, tailored look. If opting for pole or tracks, you will also have to choose a heading. Styles range from a simple gather, to the modern option of steel eyelets that allow the curtain to be threaded on the pole. The simplest way to create a pleated or gathered look is with heading tape. Rufflette headings are stocked at most department stores.

3 Using the first length as a template, cut all the fabric widths for the curtains. Start by laying the length alongside the uncut fabric. If using patterned fabrics, match the pattern along the side edges and cut the next length, trimming off any excess fabric at either end. Continue this process until you have all the lengths you need.

4 To cut plain lining fabric, straighten the edge of the fabric and cut to the same size as the curtain strips. Next, pin each fabric width together, being careful to match any pattern across the seam lines. Stitch each length together with a 1.5cm (½in) seam allowance. Having pressed the seams open stitch the lining lengths together, again pressing the seams open.

5 Lay the curtain flat the wrong side up and press a 5cm (2in) hem down both side edges and a 10cm (4in) hem along the base edges. Use pins to mark at the base edge where the side hem edge falls and mark at the side edge where the base edge falls. Unfold the hems and turn in the corner near the pins. Next, refold the hems over the turned-in corners. At this stage, you might also want to sew lead weights into each corner so that the curtains hang better.

6 Next, herringbone stitch the hems in place along the base edge and lay the curtain flat the wrong side up. Lay the lining on top, matching the top edges and pin together down the centre. Turn back the lining to one side over the pins. Lockstitch both fabrics together just above the hem. Turn back the lining over the curtains and pin together again on either side of the centre at approximately 40cm (16in) intervals. Turn back the curtain at each position and lockstitch the two fabrics together as before, repeating as necessary across the curtain. Trim off the excess lining so the raw side and base edges of the lining match the hemmed side and base edge of the curtains, Turn under 2.5cm (1in) of the lining down the side edges and pin. Next, turn up a 5cm (2in) hem on the base edge of the lining, forming neat edges and then pin. Slipstitch the lining along the side and base edge.

7 Turn down the top edges of the curtain fabric and the lining to the same width as the heading, and press. Unfold and trim off the lining to the pressed line. Turn down the fabric again and pin and tack. Position the curtain heading tape on the wrong side, just down from the top edge. Check that the triple pleats will match across the adjoining curtains (the distance between the last pleat on one and the first one on the other should be the same as the distance between the pleats).

8 At the centre edge of the curtain pull out the cords on the wrong side of the tape and knot. Turn under the tape edge in line with the curtain edge and turn down by 2cm (¾in). At the outside edge pull the cords out from the right side of the tape and leave them hanging free. Turn under the tape as before. Next, pin, tack and stitch the heading tape in place between both edges. Catch down the cords at the leading edge but leave those at the outside edge hanging free. Holding the cords together, pull fully from the outside edge to form two pleats, continuing until the curtain is the correct width. Next, knot the cord but avoid cutting off any excess as they will need to be unpleated for cleaning (the cords can be wound round a cord tidy which can be fitted into the heading tape). Then slot a hook through the heading tape behind each pleat and at each end. Finally, hang the curtains and arrange them so that they fall into open pleats.

Extracts taken from *The Pleasure of Home Furnishing* by Hilary More, courtesy of Cassell Illustrated Ltd.

MAKING A BLIND

This Roman blind is a tried-and-tested design with a simple, pared-down look. Constructed from pocketed battens sewn to the back of the blind, it is raised and lowered on strings. Velvet ribbon gives it a discreet decoration.

1 Calculate the finished length and width of the blind, adding 9cm (3½in) to the width and 10cm (4in) to the length for turnings and seam allowance. Cut out the fabric and then cut lining to the same length but 12cm (4¾in) narrower. Mark the centre of the width with a notch on both pieces. With the right sides facing, align the side edges, pin and machine-stitch, leaving a 1.5cm (½in) seam allowance down each side. Turn through to the right side and match the notches to position lining and side turnings. Press and then pin the velvet ribbon along each side of the blind. Machine the ribbon into position.

2 At the hem, turn back the raw edges by 2cm (¾in), then 3cm (1¼in). Pin and machine close to the fold to form a casing for the bottom batten. At the top, fold back a 2.5cm (1in) turning, place a length of Velcro along the top edge and machine to conceal the edges.

3 To calculate the number and position of the folds, divide the length of the finished blind by an odd number. If the blind length is 105cm (47in), divide by seven to get 15cm (6in). Working from the bottom hem, mark up 15cm (6in)

ESSENTIAL INGREDIENTS

You will need
* Fabric
* Lining
* Triple-pleat heading tape
* Curtain hooks
* Matching thread
* Lead weights
* Cord tidies
* Tic-backs

for the lower half fold. Double the number (30cm/12in) and mark the remaining full folds with chalk along the blind.

4 Cut 10cm (4in) deep strips of the lining to the original lining width. Turn in 2.5cm (1in) along each edge. Turn in 1.5cm (½in) at the ends, then fold in half along the length. Baste the open sides together to form the rod pockets. Place the folded strips on the back of the blind, aligning the basted edge of the channel to the chalk lines. Machine through all layers.

5 Measure 10cm (4in) in from the edges of the blind and mark these points on each channels. Sew rings to the edge of the fold on each one. Cut the dowelling to the lengths of the channels and bottom hem casing, and insert. Cut the batten to the width of the blind and stick Velcro along its top. Mark 10cm (4in) in from each end on the underside of the batten and attach screw eyes. Mount the batten on the wall or architrave above the window.

6 Secure a length of the blind cord to each of the bottom rings and thread up through the other rings. Mount the blind on the top batten, Velcro to Velcro. Pass blind cords through the screw eyes on the batten and pass the left-side cord along through the right-side screw eye. Pull the cords to raise the blind and form folds. Knot the ends of the cords together. Wind the cords around the cleat to secure.

SIMPLE CONTRASTING BLIND

Make a simpler blind from two contrasting fabrics. A single cord supported by two rings on tapes that hang either side of the blind raise and lower the blind that when raised support the rolled blind. Cut 1 piece from the fabrics adding 2cm (¾in) to the width and 6cm (2½in) to the depth. Lay one panel flat, wrong side up, and turn in 0.5cm (⅛in) on all four sides and then repeat for the other panel. Next, machine-stitch three sides of the two panels, wrong sides together. Insert dowelling at the bottom of the blind (machine-stitch across the blind to keep it in place). The blind should be hung from a 2.5cm (1in) wooden batten (cover the ends with fabric fixed with a staple gun). Close up the top by machine-stitching the remaining side together. Cut around 34cm (13in) of the webbing, fold in half and insert a ring in each fold. Pin each a quarter of the way from each side and staple both the blind and the webbing to the batten. Finally arrange the cord so that it will raise and lift the blind efficiently.

ESSENTIAL INGREDIENTS

The instructions for this blind are for linen blinds but you can use almost any fabric.

* As the lining won't be visible from the front, a simple white lining is perfectly suitable.
* Velvet ribbon has a luxurious look but you could use any ribbon or braid you choose.
* Stick and sew Velcro.
* Dressmakers' chalk.
* Small metal rings.
* Dowelling rod.
* Wooden batten measuring 2.5cm (1in) in cross section.
* Screw eyes.
* Blind cord.
* Cleat.

Tiling

Tiles don't just have the practical advantages of easy upkeep and cleaning, they also offer the opportunity to create a distinctive style statement.

When choosing tiles, ensure that you research and consider all the possible options, ranging from the most basic white tiles that create a clean, functional look to the glass and ceramic mosaic tiles that are far easier to apply than they at first appear.

PREPARING THE SURFACE

The glaze on tiles will highlight even the tiniest undulation in the underlying surface, so it is essential that you make sure the surface to be tiled it is not only clean and dry but also as flat as possible.

PLASTER AND PLASTERBOARD

As long as it is clean and dry, plaster and plasterboard provide the ideal surfaces for tiling. If there are any irregularities, you should smooth them out with a coat of skimming plaster. If the plaster is crumbling, however, then remove all the loose material and completely replaster the surface. If you are tiling onto plasterboard around a shower, seal it with two coats of an appropriate sealant.

PAINTED SURFACES

Because tiles won't adhere to either gloss or emulsion (latex) paint, it is essential that before tiling the surface is rubbed with a coarse abrasive paper and any loose or flaking paint is removed with a paint scraper.

WALLPAPER

Tiles should never be applied directly to any type of wallpaper or wallcovering – this should always be removed to reveal the bare plaster underneath.

EXISTING TILES

If the tiled surface is flat and in good condition it is possible to successfully tile over existing tiles. It isn't necessary to roughen them first, just ensure that the tiles are clean and dry and replace any that are badly damaged. It is also important that you ensure that joins in the new tiles don't align with those underneath.

PLYWOOD AND CHIPBOARD

Seal ordinary plywood and chipboard with PVA adhesive diluted with an equal amount of water. If you are putting up the plywood and chipboard yourself use exterior-grade products that resist damp and then the seal won't be necessary.

TOOLS OF THE TRADE

* Spirit level
* Battens
* Plumbline and bob for marking true verticals
* Masonry nails
* Pliers
* Hand-held tile cutter or platform tile cutter
* Tile saw
* Tile file
* Chinagraph pencil
* Adhesive spreader
* Small pointing trowel
* A small synthetic sponge
* Spacers (small plastic crosses used to ensure regular gaps between tiles) – alternatively you can use matchsticks

BRICKWORK

With a sufficiently thick adhesive you can tile directly onto exposed brickwork. However this is an extremely tricky job, so you may find it easier to line the walls with plasterboard first. Check that the bricks are clean and dry before dabbing them with panel adhesive every half a metre (one and a half foot) or so before pressing the plasterboard into position and leaving it to dry before tiling.

TILING A WALL

FIXING A BATTEN

The first rule of hanging tiles is that the first row should be straight. The second is that you should never trust the line of a skirting board (baseboard), the floor or the edge of a bathtub or sink. Because of this, you should always establish a bottom line that is true by lightly nailing a horizontal batten – or a series of battens – at the height of one tile from the floor. When fitting the tiles for the bottom row, you might have to cut these to fit. Always measure each successive batten with a spirit level. If you are tiling over old tiles, drill through them with a masonry bit. Fix one end of the batten to the wall and use a spirit level to ensure that it is horizontal before before fixing the other end to the wall. With a steel tape measure or a ruler, find the point at which the floor or skirting board (baseboard) is farthest from the batten. This is the lowest point of the floor. Remove the batten, put a tile against the wall at this point

and mark the tip of the tile on the wall. Replace the batten so that its top upper edge is flush with the top of the tile – but leave a gap for spacers. Use the spirit level again to confirm that the batten is horizontal. Hammer in masonry nails just far enough to hold the batten firmly in place. If you are planning to tile more than one wall, establish the lowest point of the floor and fix battens at the same height on each wall.

POSITIONING TILES ON A WALL

If the tiles don't exactly fit the width of a wall, you will have to cut pieces of tile to fill the gap. You should space the tiles so that you get a row of cut pieces at each end of the wall. It is best to configure the tiles so that cut tiles are at least half a tile's width.

Place a row of tiles on the floor close to the wall to be tiled, allowing for spacers between each tile if they are to be used. When no more tiles will fit, move the row along so that there is an equal gap at both ends – you may need to remove one tile to get a large enough gap at each end. Mark in pencil the position of the first tile in the row that will be fixed on the batten – this is where the tiling will start.

Drop a plumbline from the top of the wall through the pencil mark on the batten. Mark this true vertical on the wall. Then nail a length of batten so that it lies along the vertical line marked on the wall in order to make a right angle to the batten that is already fixed. Place a tile on the horizontal batten and press it close to the vertical one – it should fit the corner perfectly. If it doesn't, check your measurements carefully. One of the battens is probably not truly horizontal or vertical, so it will need adjusting.

FITTING TILES AROUND OBSTRUCTIONS

Make a tiling gauge by marking tile widths along the full length of a straight batten which is about four tiles wider than the obstruction (such as a window, sinks or built-in cupboard) allowing for spacers. Hold the gauge across the main window so that an equal length of gauge is overlapping on each side. There must be at least one full tile width and a gap to be filled with a cut tile on each side. Draw a pencil line on the wall to mark where the outer edges of the cut tiles will be. Hang a plumbline from whichever mark is nearer to one end of the wall. Let it drop over the batten on the wall and make a mark. With the gauge as a guide, draw tile widths on the fixed batten between the mark and the wall. Use the plumbline again and draw a true vertical through the pencil mark nearest the wall. Fix a vertical batten along the line with masonry nails, tapped in just firmly enough to hold the batten in position. Place a tile on the horizontal batten, slide it to meet the vertical one and check that it fits.

APPLYING TILES

Apply adhesive to the wall with the trowel, beginning at the point where the vertical and horizontal battens meet. Spread the adhesive as evenly as possible, keeping the depth to about 3mm ($\frac{1}{10}$in). Do not cover more than about a square metre (ten square feet) at a time. Hold the spreader at an angle of about 45 degrees and go over the adhesive so that the notches pull it into ridges, This helps to ensure that the adhesive is applied consistently and it encourages suction between the tiles and the adhesive, occasionally wiping the spreader clean on a rag. Place a tile in the corner where the two battens meet. Apply the bottom edge of the tile first and then lower the rest of it onto the adhesive. Press the tile firmly against the wall, applying equal pressure to all four corners. Position the successive tiles, pressing spacers into the gap each time to ensure that the distances are consistent. Remove the batten after 12 hours and remove the spacers (these can be reused). Next, press grout into the gaps with a small piece of sponge before using a clean sponge to wipe the surface. Finally, run a piece of dowelling over the grouting lines before cleaning the surface again.

Extracts taken from *Reader's Digest Complete DIY Manual*, courtesy of Reader's Digest Ltd.

ESTIMATING QUANTITIES

* Tiles are sold singly, in boxes containing a specified number or by the square metre or square foot. To measure the area that you plan to tile, multiply the height by the width (or the length by the width). Many suppliers will have charts that will tell you how many tiles you'll need based on the number of square metres or feet that you need (coverage is also stated on boxed sets of tiles)

* If you are going to use tiles in contrasting colours – or a combination of plain and patterned tiles – decide where you intend to put them. The best way to approach this is to make a plan on graph paper

* Because there is sometimes a slight colour variation between tiles it is important to mix up the tiles before applying them

Wallpaper

You've taken time researching and choosing the wallpaper for your room, so here's some guidance on the practical business of getting it on the wall.

PREPARING THE ROOM

Start by clearing the room, laying dust sheets and removing any wall-mounted lights, and then decorate the ceiling. If you are using a steam stripper to remove wallpaper, however, then you should paint the ceiling afterwards as steam may damage the paints. Finally, remove any old wallpaper and fill any cracks. If you are papering onto bare walls prepare the walls with glue size so that they won't absorb paste (if glue size gets onto wooden surfaces, you should remove it immediately).

MAKING PASTE AND CUTTING PAPER

Fill the bucket with the quantity of cold water specified by the manufacturer, stirring continually to avoid lumps. Then leave it to stand for around 20 minutes while you cut the paper. Measure the wall, adding around 10cm (4in) to allow for trimming. As the length of the wall is likely to be variable, measure the longest drop (if the height is very variable cut each piece as you go along). Then unroll the paper on the pasting table with the outward-facing side down. Mark the length required with a pencil (never use a pen) and cut along the line with a pair of long-bladed scissors. Continue to cut the paper. If you are using patterned paper, always match the design to the first and number the pieces so you know in which order they should be hung. Layer the cut lengths on the table and add paste, working from the centre outwards. Once you have pasted the entire piece, fold it over to halfway down each length and leave the paste to soak for as long as the manufacturer recommends. Paste more lengths in the same way while the first is soaking and leave each one to soak for the same length of time.

HANGING PAPER

Start by hanging the first length of paper on a wall that adjoins the window (work away from the largest light-source so that any overlaps won't cast shadows). If you are right-handed work in a clockwise direction, and if you are left-handed work anti-clockwise. Make a pencil mark 48cm (19in) from the corner near the top of the wall. Hold the plumbline from the mark and hang the bob so that it hangs around 1.2m (47in) down the wall and draw down its length. Press the pasted length to the top of the wall and gently unfold it with its right-hand

TOOLS OF THE TRADE

* A folding pasting table, measuring 182 x 61cm (6 x 2 ft)
* A clean 15cm (6in) paste brush
* A plastic bucket for mixing paint (tie a length of string between the ends of the handle so that you can remove surplus glue and have somewhere to rest the brush)
* 25cm (10in) wallpaper scissors
* A trimming knife
* A plumbline and bob for marking the true verticals
* A 18–25cm (7–10in) paper-hanging brush for smoothing out creases and bubbles
* If you are using pre-pasted wallpaper, you will need a water trough
* A cutting guide for trimming the edges
* Seam roller for pressing down the joins between rolls
* A sponge for removing any excess paste.

edge running down the side of the pencil mark before smoothing it in place with the paper-hanging brush. Once the end of the roll has reached the bottom of the wall, crease it into the corner with the end of the scissors or the trimming guide. Finally cut the wallaper at the top and the bottom. Repeat this procedure with the next length, aligning its edge flush with the edge of the first length and matching up any pattern carefully. Once you have hung two or three pieces, then roll the edges with a seam roller to iron out any bubbles and create a neat join.

WALLPAPERING AROUND INTERNAL CORNERS

An internal corner is one such as in the corner of a room or alcove. To wallpaper round an internal corner, start by measuring between the last length that you have hung and the corner at the top, middle and bottom of the wall. Write down the widest distance and add 13mm (½in). Cut a length of paper to this width and retain the offcut for papering the first length of the adjoining wall. Paste and hang the first length you have cut and then take the spare paper around onto the next wall. Use the brush to smooth well into the corner. Measure the offcut and hang the plumbline this distance away from the corner. Make a pencil mark down this line. Hang the offcut so that the right-hand edge aligns with the pencil marks. The length will overlap the paper that has been turned from the

previous wall. If using patterned paper, match the two pieces as closely as possible.

WALLPAPERING AROUND EXTERNAL CORNERS

An external corner is where two walls meet such as on the corners of a chimney breast. To wallpaper around an external corner, paper the wall until there is less than one width of wallpaper to the corner. Measure the distance between the edge of the last lengths and the corner at the top, middle and bottom of the wall. Add 2.5cm (1in) to allow for

the turn and cut the paper to size. Hang the length as far as the corner and take the spare paper around onto the next wall. Smooth away any bubbles with the paper-hanging brush. Then hang the offcut from the first length next to the paper on the wall, matching the pattern and butting the joins. Continue to hang lengths until you reach the internal corner. Before you paper the next wall, use the plumbline to get a vertical starting point. If the walls are irregular you might find it easier to overlap the joins rather than to butt them.

WALLPAPERING AROUND CIRCULAR LIGHT SWITCHES

Always turn off the electricity at the mains. Hang the wallpaper in the normal way until you reach the fixture. Pierce a hole in the paper over it with a pair of small scissors before cutting diagonally across the switch below. Next, mark the outline of the switch on the paper with the back of a pair of scissors, pressing the cut pieces to the switch. Cut off the surplus paper with small pointed scissors. Follow the marked outline, but allow for just a fraction of paper to turn onto the fitting so that the wall cannot show through a gap. Smooth the paper flat around the switch with a paper-hanging brush. If the paste on the paper immediately around the switch has begun to dry, apply a little more before you brush the paper flat. Then hang the rest of the length.

PAPERING AROUND SQUARE LIGHT SWITCHES AND SOCKETS

Turn off the electricity at the mains. Hang the paper from the top of the wall down as far as the switch or socket. Cut the paper to the corners of the switch and pull back the flaps. Partially unscrew the switch cover and pull it about 6mm (¼in) away from the wall. Trim away any excess paper so that around 3mm (⅛in) of paper will sit behind the cover. Gently ease the switch cover through the hole in the paper. Push the paper behind the switch cover with a piece of flat wood and then brush the paper flat against the wall, smoothing away any remaining air bubbles. Hang the remainder of the length. Rescrew the switch cover and turn on at the mains.

HANGING A BORDER

The process is similar to hanging wallpaper, however don't soak it for as long and fold it up like an accordion for easy handling. Follow the ceiling line around the room allowing around half an inch overlap on the corners. When hanging around a window or door frame overlap horizontal and vertical strips at the corners. Double cut through both strips at a 45-degree angle at the corner and remove excess pieces.

ESTIMATING QUANTITIES
----

* If using patterned wallpaper with a large repeat always buy one or two extra rolls (this is also useful if you make any mistakes). Some shops will allow you to return unused rolls. Ideally the rolls should come from the same batch, but if you have rolls from different batches use the smaller quantity in areas where any variations are less likely to be obvious.

* Most standard wallpapers are 10m x 530mm (in the US 27ft x 20½in). When measuring always use a steel tape and when calculating the perimeter of the room always include doors and windows (any excess gained in this way will be useful).

Extracts taken from *Reader's Digest Complete DIY Manual*, courtesy of Reader's Digest Ltd.

Upholstery & Soft Furnishings

Creating your own upholstery and soft furnishings will open up a whole new world – and the more you do the more proficient you'll become.

Here are a few basic projects to build your confidence to eventually take on full-scale projects.

SIMPLE ARMCHAIR COVER

1 Cut a length of the fabric for the front of the chair back and extending to the sides of the back cushion, about 7.5cm (3in) larger all round than required. Using upholstery T-pins, pin to the chair, wrong side out.

2 Cut a length of fabric for the top and side of each arm, about 7.5cm (3in) larger all round than required. Pin to the arms, wrong side out. When cutting out pieces for curved areas, snip a V along the edge every 2cm (¾in), so you can turn it out more easily.

3 Cut a piece of fabric for the seat and the drop at the front of the chair, measuring about 7.5cm (3in) larger all round than required. Pin onto the chair, wrong side out.

4 Cut two pieces for the arm fronts, extending down to align with the drop of the seat, around 5cm (2in) larger than required. Pin the fabric pieces to the arms, wrong side out.

5 For the back, cut a length of fabric, about 7.5cm (3in) larger

all round than required, matching the drop at the front and the sides. Pin on the chair, wrong side out.

6 Cut two pieces for the side, around 5cm (2in) larger all round than required. Pin onto the chair, wrong side out.

7 Trim all the excess fabric to a 1.5cm (⅝in) seam allowance. Pin the whole cover together, starting at the top. Remove the T-pins and replace with dressmakers' pins to join the pieces together. Having gone over the whole chair, carefully remove the cover. Machine-stitch the seams and remove the pins. Turn up the hem to the required length. Pin, machine-stitch and then iron.

HEADBOARD COVER

1 Make a paper template the same size as the headboard. Cut out two pieces of fabric larger than the template. Pin the template to one piece and, using dressmakers' chalk, draw a line 2.5cm (1in) outside the edge to create a seam allowance. Unpin, repeat for the remaining piece and cut along the chalked lines.

2 Cut a strip of fabric for the gusset, the length of the top and two sides, plus 2.5cm (1in)

KEY STITCHES
----

* **Herringbone stitch** This is a criss-cross stitch used to hold side hems. Working from left to right, secure the end of the thread before making an almost imperceptible back stitch in the fabric that faces outwards. As you work to the right, take a bigger back stitch through the hem.

* **Slipstitch** This is the best stitch to use when sewing a hem or two folded edges of fabric. Working from right to left, run your needle inside the folded edge for 1cm (⅜in) and then pick up one or two of the threads of the fabric that will face outward, so that the stitch will be almost invisible. When you are stitching together two folded edges, carefully and gently run the stitch inside the folded edge on one side for 1cm (⅜in) before moving over to the folded edge and running it along inside for 1cm (⅜in).

all round. Make a length of piping, using linen on the cross, to the same dimension as the gusset. Place the front panel right side up and pin piping around the sides and the top edge, lining up the raw edges.

3 Cut out eight 30 x 6cm (12 x 2¼in) strips of fabric for the ties. Fold them in half lengthways and machine the open sides together. Turn them inside out and iron flat.

4 Pin the gusset to the front panel, right sides together, so the piping is between the two pieces of fabric.

5 Slip two ties between the piping and gusset, one about a quarter of the way up from the bottom of the panel and the other three-quarters of the way up. Pin them in place. Repeat for the other side. Machine-stitch the pieces together, with a 1.5cm (½in) seam allowance. Place the back panel right-side down over the gusset, piping and ties, aligning the raw edges. Pin the corresponding ties in place. Machine-stitch together, leaving a 1.5cm (½in) allowance.

6 Pin and machine a 2cm (¾in) hem along the bottom edges of the cover. Overlock all the raw edges to prevent fraying. Turn it right side out, press and slip over the headboard. Tie the side bows.

BUTTONED CHAIR COVER

1 Pace a sheet of paper on the seat of a chair and draw around it to make a template. Still working on the paper template, extend 12cm (5in) from the seat to form the four side drops of the cover. Extend the sides of the back and ends of the side drops by 4cm (1½in) to wrap around the back of the chair leg. Round off the back corners where the fabric fits around the legs.

2 Place the template on the fabric and cut it out, adding a 1.5cm (½in) seam allowance all round. Mark a 4cm (1½in) wide back corner facing onto the template. Cut out two facings, adding a 1.5cm (½in) seam allowance.

3 Turn and machine-stitch a hem around the outside of the facing. Place the facings on the chair cover, right sides together. Pin and machine-stitch, leaving a 1.5cm (½in) seam allowance at regular intervals around the curve. Turn the facings through and press flat.

4 Pin the side drops of the front chair covers together, right sides facing. Machine-stitch leaving a 1.5cm (½in) seam allowance. Press the seams open.

5 On the right side, turn up a 1.5cm (½in) hem allowance on all sides. Pin velvet ribbon around the edge concealing the raw edges and machine-stitch in place. Machine-top-stitch around the edge of the back leg facings. Place the seat cover on the chair, wrap the extension around the back of the chair legs and mark the buttonhole positions. Machine or hand-finish the buttonholes to complete.

EDGED THROW

1 Decide on the final dimensions of the throw. Subtract 20cm (8in) from both the length and the width of the measurements. Cut the wool fabric to this size, adding a 1.5cm (½in) seam allowance all round (you may need to join pieces for a double bed).

2 Using dressmakers' chalk, mark out two strips of linen 20cm (8in) deep. Mark out the width measurements of cut wool fabric along the strip. Mark off at right angles from this measurement with a set square to form a mitre. Add a 1.5cm (½in) seam allowance all round. Repeat to give two mitred strips the same width as the fabric and two mitred strips the length of it.

3 Right sides facing, pin the corners of the linen strips together to form the border. Machine-stitch, leaving a 1.5cm (½in) seam allowance. Clip the corners.

4 Place the border right side down on the wrong side of the corresponding edge of the wool fabric. With raw edges aligned, pin and position. Machine-stitch, leaving a seam allowance of 1.5cm (½in). Repeat on all four sides.

5 Turn the corners of the border right side out and fold it over onto the right side of the wool fabric. Fold under a 1.5cm (½in) turning along the border edge. Lay ribbon along the border and machine-stitch through all layers.

PATCHWORK BEDSPREAD

1 Cut out patches from scraps of cotton and linen of the same height and varying widths. Lay the pieces out in the pattern required to get an idea of how the finished bedspread will look.

2 Starting with the first row, pin then baste the patches together, leaving a 1cm (½in) seam at the sides. Machine-stitch together. Repeat for each row. Then iron the seams out flat.

3 Pin and then baste the strips of patches together leaving a 1cm (½in) seam allowance as before. Machine-stitch all the strips together. Open out the seams and iron flat.

4 Cut long strips of velvet on the cross, each 8cm (3in) wide. Sew them together with a 1cm (½in) seam to make a length that will stretch around the outside edge of the bedspread.

5 Lay the bedspread right side up. Fold the velvet strip in half lengthways and lay it edge to edge on top of the bedspread with the open ends facing out, pleating the velvet at the corners. Pin into place. Machine-stitch 1cm (½in) in from the edge.

6 Cut the lining fabric to the size of the bedspread plus a 2cm (¾in) seam allowance. Bring the velvet edging round to the reverse side of the bedspread, turn the lining edge in 1cm (½in), and hand-hem the two together.

PIPING

* Start by making bias-cut strips by folding fabric diagonally, unfolding it and then marking parallel lines with dressmakers' chalk around 2cm (¾in) apart. To join the strips, pin together two ends so that the strips are at right angles to one another. Stitch 5mm (⅛in) in from the diagonal ends, along the straight grain and then press the seams open.

* When buying piping always ensure that it has been pre-shrunk. Taking one end of the bias strip and one end of the cord, fold the fabric over the cord with wrong sides facing and aligning the raw edges of the fabric. Finally, stitch close to the cord with thread.

Stockists

UK

FABRIC & WALLPAPER

ABBOTT & BOYD
(020) 7351 9985
www.abbottandboyd.co.uk

BAER & INGRAM
(01373) 813800
www.baer-ingram.com

BEAUMONT & FLETCHER
(020) 7352 5594
www.beaumontandfletcher.com

BUSBY & BUSBY
(01258) 881211
www.busbyfabric.com

CABBAGES & ROSES
(020) 7352 7333
www.cabbagesandroses.com

CATH KIDSTON
(020) 7935 6555; (020) 7229 8000
www.cathkidston.co.uk

CHELSEA TEXTILES
(020) 7584 0111 (fabrics);
(020) 7584 5544 (products)
www.chelseatextiles.com

CHRISTOPHER MOORE TEXTILES
(020) 8741 3699 (appointment
only) www.thetoileman.com

COLEFAX AND FOWLER
(020) 8877 6400
www.colefax.com

COLE & SON
(020) 7376 4628
www.cole-and-son.com

DENIM IN STYLE
(01666) 500051
www.deniminstyle.co.uk

DESIGNERS GUILD
(020) 7351 5775
www.designersguild.com

G P & J BAKER
(01202) 266700
www.gpjbaker.com

JEAN MONRO
(020) 8971 1712
www.jeanmonro.co.uk

JOHN LEWIS
0845 604 9049
www.johnlewis.com

LAURA ASHLEY
0870 562 2116
www.lauraashley.com

LEE JOFA
(01202) 266800
www.leejofa.com

LEWIS & WOOD
(01453) 860080
www.lewisandwood.co.uk

THE NATURAL FABRIC COMPANY
(01295) 730064
www.naturalfabriccompany.com

OSBORNE & LITTLE
(020) 7352 1456
www.osborneandlittle.com

RALPH LAUREN HOME
(020) 7535 4600
www.rlhome.polo.com

ROMO
(01623) 756699
www.romofabrics.com

SANDBERG
0800 967222
www.sandbergtapeter.com

SANDERSON
(01895) 830044
www.sanderson-uk.com

WARNER FABRICS
(020) 8971 1713
www.warnerfabrics.com

ZOFFANY
0870 830 0350
www.zoffany.com

FLOORING

ALLIED CARPETS
08000 932932
www.alliedcarpets.co.uk

THE ALTERNATIVE FLOORING COMPANY
(01264) 335111
www.alternativeflooring.com

AMTICO
0800 667766
www.amtico.com

BLENHEIM CARPETS
(020) 7823 6333
www.blenheim-carpets.com

B&Q
0845 222 1000
www.diy.com

BRUCE HARDWOOD FLOORS
(02476) 321131
www.bruce.com

CORMAR CARPETS
(01204) 881234
www.cormarcarpets.co.uk

DALSOUPLE
(01278) 727 733
www.dalsouple.com

DOMUS TILES
(020) 7091 1500
www.domustiles.com

JOHN LEWIS
0845 604 9049;
www.johnlewis.com

JUNCKERS
(01376) 534 700
www.junckershardwood.com

PARIS CERAMICS
(020) 7371 7778
www.parisceramics.com

THE NATURAL FLOOR COMPANY
(01737) 823666
www.thenaturalfloorcompany.com

THE NATURAL WOOD FLOOR COMPANY
(020) 8871 9771
www.naturalwoodfloor.co.uk.

ORIGINAL STONE COMPANY
(01283) 501090
www.originalstoneco.co.uk

QUICK-STEP
(00 32) 56 67 52 11
www.quick-step.com

SINCLAIR TILL
(020) 7720 0031
www.sinclairtill.co.uk

STONE AGE
(020) 7384 9090
www.estone.co.uk

TERRA FIRMA TILES
(020) 7485 7227
www.terrafirmatiles.co.uk

ULSTER CARPETS
(0808) 1000979
www.ulstercarpets.com

WORLD'S END TILES
(020) 7819 2100
www.worldsendtiles.co.uk

LIGHTING

BELLA FIGURA
(020) 7376 4564; 07000 235523
www.bella-figura.co.uk

BEST AND LLOYD
(01214) 556400
www.bestandlloyd.co.uk

CHRISTOPHER WRAY LIGHTING
(020) 7751 8701
www.christopherwray.com

GEOFFREY HARRIS LIGHTING
(020) 7228 6101
www.geoffreyharris.co.uk

JOHN CULLEN LIGHTING
(020) 7371 5400
www.johncullenlighting.co.uk

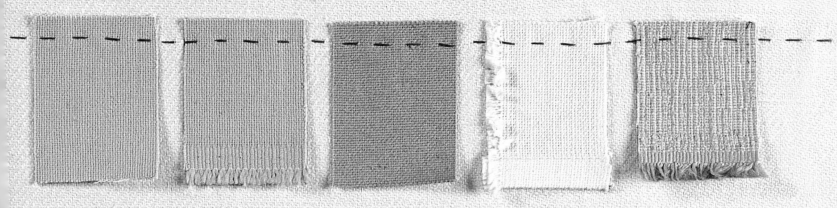

LAURA ASHLEY
0870 562 2116
www.lauraashley.com

THE LIGHTING AGENCY
(01252) 719192
www.lightingagency.co.uk

LONDON LIGHTING COMPANY
(020)7589 3612
www.londonlighting.co.uk

MARKS & SPENCER
0845 302 1234 or 0845 603 1603
www.marksandspencer.com

STIFFKEY LAMPSHOP
(01328) 830460
www.stiffkeylampshop.co.uk

PAINT

CROWN
(01254) 704951
www.crownpaint.co.uk

CROWN TRADE PAINTS
(01254) 704951
www.historic-colours.co.uk

FARROW & BALL
(01202) 876141
www.farrow-ball.com

FIRED EARTH
(01295) 812088; (01295) 814300
www.firedearth.com

FRANCESCA'S PAINTS
(020) 7228 7694
www.francescaspaint.com

INTERNATIONAL PAINTS
(01480) 484284
www.international-paints.co.uk

JOHN OLIVER
(020) 7221 6466
www.johnoliver.co.uk

LEYLAND PAINTS
(01924) 354000
www.leylanddsm.co.uk

**THE LITTLE GREENE
PAINT COMPANY**
(0161) 230 0880
www.thelittlegreene.com.

PAINT & PAPER LIBRARY
(020) 7823 7755
www.paintlibrary.co.uk

PAPERS AND PAINTS
(020) 7352 8626;
colourman.com

RENDONA PAINTS
(01291) 620351
rendona.co.uk

ROSE OF JERICHO
(01935) 83676
www.rose-of-jericho.demon.co.uk

US

FABRIC &
WALLPAPER

**THE CLAREMONT FURNISHING
FABRICS CO. INC**
212-486-1252
www.claremontfurnishing.com

FABRIC MART
Toll-Free: 800-242-3695
www.fabricmartfabrics.com

HOUSEFABRIC.COM
314-968-0090
www.housefabric.com

LEE JOFA INC.
516-752-7600
www.leejofa.com

SCALAMANDRÉ
631-467-8800
www.scalamandre.com

F & B SPECIALTY LINENS
Toll-Free: 800-268-2993
www.fblinen.com

FRENCH QUARTER LINENS
Toll-Free: 1-888-200-7498
www.eurolinens.com

GARNET HILL
Toll-Free: 1-888-842-9696
www.garnethill.com

THE LINEN PLACE
212-629-0300
Toll-Free: 1-866-629-0300
www.linenplace.com

TEXTILE SHOP
Toll-Free: 1-877-839-7467
www.textileshop.com

**BRADBURY & BRADBURY
ART WALLPAPER**
707-746-1900
www.bradbury.com

CHESAPEAKE WALLCOVERINGS
301-249-7900
Toll-Free: 800-275-2037
www.cheswall.com

HARLEQUIN USA
678-303-9999
www.harlequin.uk.com

LAURA ASHLEY
www.laura-ashley.com

WAVERLY
Toll-Free: 800-275-2037
www.waverly.com

YORK WALLPAPER AND FABRICS
Toll-Free: 800-455-9913
www.yorkwall.com

FLOORING

AMTICO INTERNATIONAL INC.
404-267-1900
www.amtico.com

ARMSTRONG FLOORS
Toll-Free: 800-233-3823
www.armstrong.com

BRUCE HARDWOOD FLOORS
214-887-2000
Toll-Free: 800-722-4647
www.armstrong.com/resbrucew
oodna/index

CARPET INNOVATIONS
212-966-9440
www.carpetinnovations.com

CROSSVILLE PORCELAIN STONE
931-484-2110
www.crossville-ceramics.com

MODERN RUGS
Toll-Free: 1-800-830-RUGS
www.modernrugs.com

PARIS CERAMICS
212-644-2782
www.parisceramics.com

LIGHTING

FABBY LIGHTING
323-939-1388
www.fabby.com

HINKLEY LIGHTING
216-671-3300
Toll-Free: 800-446-5539
www.hinkleylighting.com

LAMPSPLUS.COM
www.lampsplus.com

LIGHTING UNIVERSE
www.lightinguniverse.com

PAINT

CABOT STAINS
800-877-8246
Toll-free: 1-800-US-STAIN
www.cabotstain.com

OLD VILLAGE PAINTS
610-238-9001
www.old-village.com

PRATT & LAMBERT PAINTS
Toll-Free: 800-289-7728
www.prattandlambert.com

Index

Acknowledgments

All photographs are the copyright of Homes & Gardens magazine/IPC Media and the publisher wishes to acknowledge the following photographers: P.1 Jake Curtis; P.2 Tim Winter; P.5 Simon Upton; P.6 Niall McDiarmid; P.9 Jake Curtis; P.10 Pia Tryde; P.12 Nicolas Bruant; P.13 Jo Fairclough; P.14 left Tim Young; P.14 right Edina van der Wyck; P.15 Paul Zammit/St John Pope; P.16 Pia Tryde; P.17 left David Palmer; P.17 right James Merrell; P.18 Niall McDirmid; P.19 Harry Cory-Wright; P.20 Polly Wreford; P.21 left Polly Wreford; P.21 right Pia Tryde; P.22 Tom Leighton; P.23 left Caroline Arber; P.23 right Tom Leighton; P.24 Jo Fairclough; P.25 Simon Upton; P.26 Catherine Gratwicke; P.27 Christopher Drake; P.28 Polly Wreford; P.29 Tom Leighton; P.30 Caroline Arber; P.31 left and right Peter Campbell Saunders; P.32–33 Paul Zammit; P.33 right Andrew Wood; P.34 left Brian Harrison; P.34 right Catherine Gratwicke; P.35 Jan Baldwin; P.36 Claudia Dulak; P.38 Jan Baldwin; P.39 Jan Baldwin; P.40 left Debi Treloar; P.40 right Debi Treloar; P.41 above and below Paul Zammit; P.42 Andrew Wood; P.43 Peter Campbell Saunders; P.44 Paul Bowden; P.45 Marc Broussard; P.46–7 above Claudia Dulak; P.46–7 below Tom Leighton; P.48 Emma Lee; P.50 Jan Baldwin; P.51 Paul Massey/Living Etc; P.52 above Pia Tryde; P.52 below Kim Sayer; P.53 Pia Tryde; P.55 Caroline Arber; P.57 Simon Brown; P.58 left Debi Treloar; P.58–59 Mark Williams; P.60 left Tim Young; P.60 right Simon Upton; P.62 Geoffrey Young; P.63 Caroline Arber; P.64 left Tom Leighton; P.64 right John Mason; P.65 Jan Baldwin; P.66 Tim Winter; P.67 left Craig Fordham; P.67 right Jan Baldwin; P.68 Peter Campbell Saunders; P.70 Simon Whitmore; P.71 Simon Whitmore; P.72 left Andrew Wood; P.72 right Simon Whitmore; P.73 Tim Young; P.74 Jo Fairclough; P.75 left Polly Eltes; P.75 right Hotze Eisma; P.76 left Adrian Briscoe; P.76 right Caroline Arber; P.77 Tom Stewart; P.78 Jan Baldwin; P.79 James Merrell; P.80 Jan Baldwin; P.81 Andreas von Einsiedel; P.82 Edina van der Wyck; P.83 left and right Simon Bevan; P.84 Peter Campbell Saunders; P.86 Winfried Heinze; P.87 left Jan Baldwin; P.87 right Jan Baldwin; P.88–89 Pia Tryde; P.90 above Niall McDiarmid; P.90 below Edina van der Wyck; P.91 Caroline Arber; P.92 Pia Tryde; P.93 Paul Zammit; P.94 Robin Mathews; P.95 Christopher Beckett; P.96 Debi Treloar; P.97 left John Mason; P.97 right Winfried Heinze/Living Etc; P.98 Sandra Lane; P.100 Tom Leighton; P.101 David Montgomery; P.102 left David Montgomery; P.102 right Niall McDiarmid; P.103 Polly Wreford; P.104 above Jake Curtis; P.104 below Andrew Wood; P.105 Caroline Arber; P.106 Caroline Arber; P.107 Jake Curtis; P.108 right Jo Tyler; P.108–109 David Brittain; P.110 Emma Lee; P.112 Caroline Arber; P.113 J P Masclet/Living Etc; P.114 Andrew Wood; P.115 left Polly Wreford; P.115 right Paul Massey; P.116–7 Tom Leighton; P.117 right Edina van der Wyck; P.118 left David Montgomery; P.118–9 Caroline Arber; P.120 above Tim Young; P.120 below Polly Wreford; P.121 Tim Young; P.122–123 Polly Wreford; P.126–7 above Paul Zammit; P.126–7 below Caroline Arber; P.127 above right David Still; P.127 below right Paul Massey; P.128 above Andreas von Einsiedel; P.128 below Winfried Heinze; P.130 –131 Paul Zammit; P.132–3 Spike Powell; P.133 right Debi Treloar; P.134 Kim Sayer; P.135 Alex Ramsay; P.136–137 Catherine Gratwicke; P.138 Jo Tyler; P.138–139 Jan Baldwin; P.140 Elizabeth Zechin; P.141 Jan Baldwin; P.142–3 Polly Wreford; P.144–5 Tim Young; P.146 above Jan Baldwin; P.146 below Caroline Arber; P.147 above Polly Wreford; P.147 below Tom Leighton; P.148–9 Tom Leighton; P.149 right Simon Upton; P.150–151 Christopher Drake; P.152–3 Tom Leighton; P.154 Jake Fitzjones/Living Etc; P.155 above Andrew Wood; P.155 below David Garcia; P.156–7 Niall McDiarmid; P.158–9 Christopher Drake; P.160 Christopher Drake; P.161 above Jan Baldwin; P.161 below Winfried Heinze; P.162–163 Paul Massey; P.164 Emma Lee; P.167 Claudia Dulak; P.169 Emma Lee; P.171 Edina van der Wyck; P.173 Peter Campbell Saunders; P.175 Tham Nhu Tran; P.177 Alun Callender; P.178 Tim Young; P.181 Polly Eltes; P.182 Jan Baldwin; P.185 Peter Campbell Saunders; P.187 Paul Bowden; P.188–189 Jake Curtis; P.190–1 Peter Campbell Saunders; P.192 Peter Campbell Saunders.

The publisher wishes to thank the following photographers, agencies and companies for their kind permission to reproduce the following photographs: P.54 Crown Paints; P.56 Romo Fabrics; P.61 Andreas von Einsiedel; P.124–125 Plain English; P.129 Plain English.

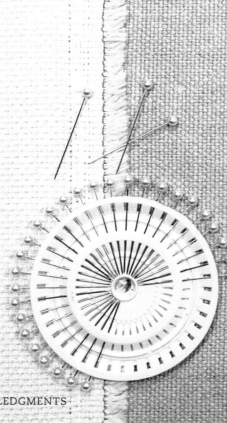